ARE YOU FIT FOR LIFE?

ARE YOU FIT FOR LIFE?

JACK GRAHAM

CROSSWAY BOOKS
WHEATON, ILLINOIS

Library of Congress Cataloging-in-Publication Data
Graham, Jack, 1950–
  Are you fit for life? / Jack Graham.
    p. cm.
  ISBN 13: 978-1-58134-912-2 (hc)
  1. Christian life. I. Title.
BV4501.3.G725   2007
248.4—dc22   2007027974

LB		18	17	16	15	14	13	12	11	10	09	08
15	14	13	12	11	10	9	8	7	6	5	4	3	2	1

To

DR. KENNETH COOPER

*The Father of Aerobics, physician, friend, and
fellow runner in the race of life. With deep gratitude for
your Christian influence, churchmanship, and sincere devotion to
the Savior. Your healing words and passionate work
have changed the world.*

Contents

Acknowledgments

I want to express my deep appreciation to the following people for their support of this project.

To Phil Rawley, editor, who always gives clarity to my words.

To my friends at Crossway Books for your support and encouragement. Thank you for believing in me as an author.

To Scott Seal and our team at PowerPoint Ministries for your help in delivering the message around the world.

To our incredible ministerial staff at Prestonwood Baptist Church as you faithfully guide our congregation in the witness of the gospel.

To Deb Graham, whose love blesses my life every single day.

Most of all, to Jesus, the Lord of my life, the One who makes it all worthwhile.

Introduction

Are you fit for life? That is a question we should all answer. Physical fitness is now one of the major priorities of millions of people, and exercise is now an international pastime. In 1968 Dr. Kenneth Cooper launched a fitness revolution with his classic book *Aerobics*. Since those days, millions of people have laced up their shoes and hit the streets and gyms in pursuit of wellness. Certainly we now know the value of exercise. Running, walking, lifting, or cycling has become a way of life for men and women of all ages. The goal is a lifetime of great health and the happiness that goes along with it. We know that the quality of life is definitively improved when we consistently practice good health habits, which include proper nutrition, regular exercise, and conditioning. If you are physically fit, you are much less likely to die prematurely than those who are unfit.

Your mental and emotional health is also dramatically improved. If you exercise regularly, you are less likely to be depressed and anxious. The stress of daily life is burned off, and the "feel good" chemicals of the brain are enhanced. Age-related decline can be slowed, including mental functioning. So without a doubt we should all get off the couch and begin moving. But, of course, there is more to life than being physically fit. God created us body, soul, and spirit, and therefore we must take care of the mind as well as the body and the spirit.

Scripture says we are to be spiritually fit so that we may live in wholeness.

> May God himself, the God who makes everything holy and whole, make you holy and whole, put you together—spirit, soul, and body—and keep you fit for the coming of our Master, Jesus Christ. The One who called you is completely dependable. If he said it, he'll do it! (1 Thessalonians 5:23–24, The Message)

Too many Christians are unfit for the challenges of life. While we have been given life in Christ, we have often failed to live in the fullness of His power. Too many of us are trudging through life without passion, unsure of our purpose and unlikely to make a difference for the Kingdom of God. Somehow we have chosen to merely exist rather than really live. What a shame since Jesus Himself promised us an abundant life:

> The thief comes only to steal and kill and destroy. I came that they may have life and have it abundantly. (John 10:10)

Yes, you can and should be spiritually, emotionally, intellectually, socially, and physically *fit for life*. That is what this book is about. The Bible is the Book of Life and gives us clear guidance as to how God intends for us to live.

There is a letter in the New Testament—Philippians—that is all about the promise and provision of this abundant life. Written by the greatest Christian who ever lived, it is all about a life that wins. As a matter of fact, the author, Paul, gives us the theme when he writes:

> For to me to live is Christ, and to die is gain. (Philippians 1:21)

To be ready to live and ready to die should be the ambition of every follower of Christ, and the message of Philippians tells us how to receive and achieve this Christ-honoring goal. Written from prison, this small book of four chapters contains the promises and principles of joyful, grateful, confident living whatever circumstances or conditions we face.

This life is for you. You can live with an outrageous optimism that says,

> I can do all things through him [Christ] who strengthens me. (Philippians 4:13)

Are you fit for life? The question is a good one. I hope to help you answer it and to discover this life in Christ that will transform your every day into an exciting adventure of faith and fullness. So let's get moving and start enjoying this life right now.

PART ONE

Gearing Up

CHAPTER ONE

What Matters Most

You may remember a time when our nation's obsession with fitness was considered a craze, just a fad. The media even used the term *fitness craze* to describe what was then a new trend in terms of people's awareness about the importance of being fit and their determination to eat a healthy diet and exercise regularly.

Well, I think you'll agree with me that America's obsession with fitness is more than a passing fad. In fact, it has gone from a passing fad to passing legislation, as New York City did with its new law to ban the serving of trans fats in its restaurants. We also have evidence of the seriousness of this commitment to fitness. As I write this, the cancer center at one of Dallas's largest hospitals is setting up a workout center in what used to be just a reading room full of literature on cancer and the various treatments available.

A cancer patient who noticed all of the expensive new workout equipment—which included treadmills, step climbers, stationary bikes, and a scale—asked her physician what was happening. The physician explained that the doctors had donated their own money to purchase the equipment and were going to offer free exercise and diet classes to help their patients get into shape. That's a great thing, because for cancer patients being fit is not only a good option to being out of shape or overweight—it can help them fight and survive their disease.

The truth is that being fit for life is a serious matter for all of us. And the good news is that the Bible has a life-changing message for us on this issue, because no one is more concerned about our physical, mental, emotional, and spiritual fitness than the God who made us and redeemed us. He even gave us a "fitness manual" in His Word—the apostle Paul's letter to his beloved friends at the church he founded in Philippi. My purpose in this book is to help you understand and apply the truths of the book of Philippians in a way that will truly help you be fit for life.

Most of us aren't accustomed to thinking of Paul as a fitness guru. But he was, at least according to the definition of fitness I gave you above. For instance, it was Paul who taught us that our bodies are the temple of the Holy Spirit (1 Corinthians 6:19) and therefore not to be defiled. And Paul took his own advice as a man who disciplined his physical appetites so he wouldn't fall into sin and be disqualified from receiving God's prize (1 Corinthians 9:24–27).

Paul also understood the importance of good emotional fitness, thanking the "God of all comfort" (2 Corinthians 1:3) for the way He comforted and sustained him in all of his trials. Paul is often characterized as a hard-driving, Type A personality who didn't let anything bother him. But as we'll see, he was a very tenderhearted man who loved his fellow Christians like a father. In fact, the book of Philippians is something of a spiritual valentine, if you will, in which Paul expressed his deep love and affection for believers serving Christ in a very important region of the world.

Paul was also intellectually fit. He was a scholar of the first rank, and his exhortation to Timothy has become the goal of every sincere servant of God: "Study to show thyself approved unto God, a workman that needeth not to be ashamed, rightly dividing the word of truth" (2 Timothy 2:15, KJV). To the great apostle, the Christian faith was a body of teaching to be studied, diligently absorbed into the mind, and taught with faithfulness and accuracy. Paul's entire ministry of proclaiming the gospel of Jesus Christ serves as evidence for his concern for spiritual fitness.

The physical circumstances under which Paul wrote to the Philippians are worth mentioning because he was in a place that was nothing but harmful to his health. He wrote this letter from a Roman prison—a filthy dungeon with zero physical comforts. He was in a damp, dark, cold cell and was probably chained to the wall as well. But even though Paul was, many Bible scholars believe, a rather small, slightly built, middle-aged man with physical problems, he was far more fit for life than the physically fit Roman soldiers who guarded him. So he has much to say about being fit for life.

If we are going to be at our best, we need to get into the best physical, emotional, mental, and spiritual shape possible. The place to begin is with our relationships—with Jesus Christ first of all and then with family and friends and the fellowship of God's church. Paul knew what matters most. So he began his letter to the Philippians by identifying both himself and his readers in terms of their relationship with Christ: "Paul and Timothy, servants of Christ Jesus, to all the saints in Christ Jesus who are at Philippi" (1:1–2).

YOUR RELATIONSHIP WITH JESUS CHRIST

Paul identifies himself as a "servant," or slave, of Christ. The apostle was so totally sold out to Jesus that he could say, "for to me to live is Christ, and to die is gain" (Philippians 1:21). This is a critical point for all believers. Everything in life begins here. Jesus is our very life, and we are to serve Him because He has captured our hearts.

To become a child of God, you *do* have to become a saint. Most people have been conditioned to think that a saint is someone who has achieved a lofty spiritual status or has been canonized for doing good works or even performing miracles. But that's not how the Bible uses this word. A saint is simply a true believer, a person who has been born into the family of God through faith in Jesus Christ.

Therefore saints aren't made, they're born from above in the new birth. That's why we can say when it comes to your relationship with Christ, you're either a saint or you ain't. The word *saint* means "a set apart one," a person who has been chosen by God and called for His purposes. This applies to every believer. So instead of being something mystical or super-spiritual, *saint* is a very basic description of our life in Christ. God has set us aside for an eternal purpose, which means we can live with passion.

What matters most of all, then, is whether you have trusted Christ and His finished work on the cross for your salvation or whether you are trying to please God by being a good person. If it's the latter, I urge you to put this book down right now and trust Christ alone to forgive your sins and come into your life and give you eternal life—and He will! Trying to be fit for life without knowing Jesus as your Savior is like trying to work out while wearing shoes and gym clothes that are about three sizes too small. Life will never work out without Jesus.

YOUR RELATIONSHIP WITH OTHERS

The recipients of Paul's letter in Philippi were true saints of God, Paul's own spiritual children whom he had led to Christ. So he writes to them with genuine affection:

> Grace to you and peace from God our Father and the Lord Jesus Christ. I thank my God in all my remembrance of you, always in every prayer of mine for you all making my prayer with joy, because of your partnership in the gospel from the first day until now. And I am sure of this, that he who began a good work in you will bring it to completion at the day of Jesus Christ. It is right for me to feel this way about you all, because I hold you in my heart, for you are all partakers with me of grace, both in my imprisonment and in the defense and confirmation of the gospel. For God is my witness, how I yearn for you all with the affection of Christ Jesus. (Philippians 1:2–8)

These Christians were on Paul's mind and in his heart. He understood the importance of the love relationship we are to have with one another in the church, the body of Christ. When you belong to Christ, you also belong to everyone else who belongs to Christ.

The sooner we realize that we can't go it alone, the better off we're going to be because the Christian life was never meant to be a solo act. Millions have watched the television program *American Idol*. Early on in the competition there is a tryout phase. The vast majority of the thousands of people they bring onto the stage can't sing at all. After hearing them, the question that comes to the mind of the viewer is, "Where did these people get the idea that they could sing?"

The contestants on *American Idol* are trying to go it alone, and a few make it. But while performing solo may be okay for a musical career, it's no way to live. The work of Jesus Christ advances on a network of relationships among believers who are partners in life. It is because of our fellowship in Christ that we are able to advance the gospel to the world. Without a doubt, the people who make the greatest difference for Christ are the people who know how to love Him and other people with all their hearts.

Paul basically told his friends at Philippi, "I thank God every time I think about you" (1:3). I wonder what our fellow believers say when they think about us. Do they thank God for us because of our love and commitment?

Do you seek healthy relationships by loving and serving others more than yourself? That's a pretty convicting question, and someone might respond, "You don't know the kind of people I have to put up with in my life. They aren't all nice, lovable people like the saints at Philippi probably were." I know people can be difficult, and even our friends at church can be exasperating at times.

The church of Jesus Christ is a real blend of people from all strata and seasons of life. But it's always been that way. Consider the people at Philippi. Acts 16:11–40 is the story of Paul's first visit to this Roman province in Macedonia and the founding of the church there.

The first conversion in Philippi was that of Lydia, a wealthy businesswoman who became a follower of Jesus along with her household (vv. 13–15). Another new believer was a demonized slave girl who was being used by her masters to bring in a profit by fortune-telling (vv. 16–19). Then a hardened Roman jailer was miraculously transformed by God's grace, and he and his entire family believed and were baptized (vv. 31–34).

This sampling of the church represents a broad cross section of people who have one thing in common—their relationship with Jesus Christ.

These very different men, women, and children were now in the spiritual family of Jesus Christ. This is the church, God's family together in Christ. Note the emphasis on the local church in this passage. The New Testament teaches the universal brotherhood of believers, the worldwide family of God. But sometimes it's easier to love your brothers and sisters on the other side of the world, whom you've never met, than it is to love those on the other side of the church aisle whom you meet every week. While we are part of the church global, we are to experience the church local.

My point is that the Bible doesn't let us hide behind the idea of, "Oh yes, I love the body of Christ around the world" while we're not relating properly to the people in our own community of faith. At least 90 percent of the time the New Testament uses the term *church* in reference to a specific local body of believers. Paul didn't just write to the church at large, but to the churches in Philippi, Ephesus, Corinth, Galatia, and so on.

The two things emphasized in Philippians 1:2–8 were the love and affection of God's people for one another and their witness of the gospel. When it comes right down to it, love is what matters most because Jesus said that "the great and first commandment" is to "love the Lord your God with all your heart and with all your soul and with all your mind." Then He gave the second most important commandment: "love your neighbor as yourself" (Matthew 22:37–39). Jesus concluded this teaching by saying in verse 40, "On these two commandments depend all the Law and the Prophets." This is what matters most.

Jesus was summarizing the heart of the Ten Commandments (Exodus 20:1–17) and all of the Old Testament Law. The first four of the Ten Commandments have to do with our love for God, and the next six have to do with our love for and relationships with others. Loving God and one another in Christ is the essence of faith.

That same love extends to the world as we care about people who need Jesus in their lives. We need to understand that true ministry flows from sacrificial love. The love of Christ had changed Paul's life so dramatically that he gladly called himself a servant, or slave, of Christ (Philippians 1:1). It was out of the overflow of Paul's love for Christ that he poured out his life in service to Christ and to others, and he did it with intense devotion. Paul also learned how to receive the love and ministry of others in the family of faith, and he rejoiced in it.

I rejoiced in the Lord greatly that now at length you have revived your concern for me. You were indeed concerned for me, but you had no opportunity. (Philippians 4:10)

Unlike your biological family, you can choose your church family—but it will have the same strengths and flaws as your own family. So if you're unhappy with your church because it's full of imperfect people and you think you can get a better deal down the road, you may find yourself very disappointed.

A man was so sick and tired of the people in his town that he packed up and left. He drove down the road a little bit and entered a town that seemed like a nice place to live. An old man was sitting on the steps of the city hall. So the traveler rolled down the window of his car and called out, "Hey, I'm thinking about moving here. What are the people like in this town?"

The old gentleman said, "Well, I don't know. What were the people like in the town you came from?"

"Oh," the man replied, "they were terrible, awful, the worst people I've ever been around."

The old man looked at him and smiled. "You know what? The people in this town are just like that too, so you better go on farther down the road."

I don't know what your church is like, but I do know that God has placed you there for a reason. And unless and until He moves you on, that's where God wants you to serve in the fellowship of Christ's body. If you want to get fit, every part of the body has to cooperate.

I spent some extra time discussing our spiritual relationships because they are so important to the fitness for life that this book examines.

There is no question that your family relationships also play a vital role in getting fit for life. How you express your love is very important. Bobby Bowden, the famous coach of the Florida State University Seminoles, was asked by his wife, "Honey, do you love me more than football?"

Bowden thought for a minute and said, "College or pro?"

That's not the way to do it! Men are notorious for not showing and sharing their love and for having an "I want to be served" attitude. But even Jesus did not come to be served but to serve (Mark 10:45), and that's the attitude we are to express in our families.

One problem in family relationships that also occurs in our church relationships is unrealistic expectations. Have you heard about Husband-

Mart? In this fictional store a woman can choose her ideal husband from many options. The store has six floors, and the men increase in positive attributes as the shopper ascends each flight. But there is a catch, because once a shopper decides to leave a floor and go up to the next one, she can't go back down except to exit the building.

So one woman comes to the Husband-Mart to find a husband. On the first floor, the sign on the door reads, "These men have jobs!" The woman says, "Well, that's better than my last boyfriend, but I wonder what's available further up?"

So up the elevator she goes to the second floor, where the sign reads, "These men have jobs and love kids." The woman likes this because she wants to have a family. But she also figures that if it's this good already, it can only get better. Sure enough, the third-floor sign says, "These men have jobs, love kids, and are extremely good-looking." Now the woman is really getting excited, but she figures it will only keep getting better.

So she heads on up to the fourth floor, where the sign says, "These men have jobs, love kids, are extremely good-looking, and help with the housework."

"Incredible!" the woman exclaims. "This is very tempting, but there must be something even better on the fifth floor," and she keeps moving up. To her delight, the fifth floor is better: "These men have jobs, love kids, are extremely good-looking, help with the housework, and have a strong romantic streak."

Well, by now this woman is so ecstatic that she thinks to herself, *Just imagine what must be waiting for me on the last floor!* So up to the sixth floor she goes and steps out of the elevator with great excitement, only to be greeted with this sign: "You are visitor number 3,456,789,012. There are no men on this floor. This floor exists solely as proof that women are impossible to please. Thank you for shopping at Husband-Mart."

The Husband-Mart, or the Wife- or Child-Mart for that matter, would be a good joke if it weren't so true. Developing healthy relationships in your family is much like developing a healthy body through exercise. You have to start where you are, set realistic goals for progress, and then work faithfully with what you've got to get from where you are to where you want to be. Start expecting the best from the people you love, and watch your relationships develop.

I use the term *marketplace* to describe our relationships in business and public life because it has a wider connotation than business alone. You don't have to have a job or own a business to relate to people in the marketplace. The apostle Paul was also conscious of the importance of these relationships as he instructed believers how to be fit for life. He wrote to the Philippians, "Let your manner of life be worthy of the gospel of Christ" (1:27).

Many people tend to think of good relationships in this arena as secondary to success in business or some other area of public life. But not so. Zig Ziglar included an interesting quote in his book *Top Performance*. The former CEO of Coca-Cola, who was responsible for taking the company from a regional business to an international powerhouse, is quoted as saying:

> Success or failure on the job is essentially a matter of relationships, and the deadly sin in our relationship with people is that we take them for granted. We do not make an active or continuous effort to do and say things that will make them like us and believe us, and that will create in them the desire to work with us in the attainment of our desires and purposes.

In business, good relationships make all the difference. Whether you work in a company, operate a business of your own, or simply relate to people each day in carrying out your personal or family business, it matters to God how you conduct yourself and the witness you leave. We call these *people skills* because relating well to others is a skill we should learn if we really want to get fit for life.

How to Grow in Your Relationships

When we get to the end of our lives, it's not our diplomas, trophies, or stock portfolio that will comfort us. We will want our family and friends—people to be with us—because what matters most in life and death are the people we love and who love us. Here are several ways you can cultivate and nurture your relationships so that your life will be full and fulfilling.

Grow in Christ

The place to begin nurturing your relationships is with Jesus. You can live with confidence, knowing that your relationship with Christ is secure forever.

"He who began a good work in you will bring it to completion at the day of Jesus Christ" (Philippians 1:6). That's an eternal promise you can trust every day. When Christ comes for you, be prepared for that moment and for your life with Him in heaven.

How is this possible? Not because of what we have done, but because of what Christ is doing in us. God always finishes what He starts, and because God has started the good work of salvation in you, He will bring it to completion. This should give you real hope as you seek to grow in your relationship to Christ through His Word, prayer, worship, service, witnessing, and the other disciplines of the Christian life. Do we fail and feel like giving up sometimes? Of course we do. But the promise of God's Word is that He will never give up on us.

Now understand that it takes patience to grow in Christ. I love the commercial of an overweight man who goes to the gym to get in shape. He gets on the scales to check his weight, gets off and runs around the room for a few seconds, then steps back on the scales and sighs when he sees that he hasn't lost any weight.

That's often the way we are in our relationship with Christ. We jog through a few Bible verses a couple of times a week, shoot up a quick prayer or two, and then wonder why we're not in better spiritual shape. But God's plan for us, like a good exercise and diet plan for our bodies, involves daily discipline. Stay with it, and soon people will be saying to you, "You're different; you've changed. God must be doing something in your life."

Grow in Your Love

If you get nothing else from this book, I pray you will make the discovery that the Christian life is not a self-improvement or do-it-yourself project, but a matter of allowing Christ to take control of your life. The real joy is growing in Christ and communing with Him in a growing relationship of love and intimacy. That's what God desires for you.

Paul prayed that the love of the Philippians would "abound more and more" (1:9).

Love that abounds is love that overflows to others. The difference between the love taught in the Bible and the kind the world talks about is that the love of Christ is a choice of the will, not simply a warm, fuzzy feeling we can't control. You don't fall in love accidentally. You grow in love toward God and toward others as a decision of your will.

Guard Your Mind

Another way to grow in your relationships is to guard your mind. For instance, even as we show love freely to others, it is not to be foolishly or blindly given. After Paul prayed that the Philippians might have abounding love, he added, "with knowledge and all discernment" (1:9). Our love for Christ includes loving the truth. Love that is out of control does not become a flowing river of blessing but a stagnant swamp. The two banks between which the river of our love must flow are knowledge and discernment.

The world sings songs that ask, "How can it be wrong when it feels so right?" But the answer of God's Word is that love or anything else can be wrong if it goes outside the boundaries of God's will and God's Word. As we relate to God and to others in love, we need to make sure that our love is according to the truth. When you give your heart, that doesn't mean you lose your head. Nor do we ever compromise God's Word in the name of love.

Give Your Best

Paul ended the first section of Philippians 1 with these words: "So that you may approve what is excellent, and so be pure and blameless for the day of Christ, filled with the fruit of righteousness that comes through Jesus Christ, to the glory and praise of God" (vv. 10–11).

These verses speak of the importance of excellence in what we do for Christ, both in our personal lives and as we relate to others. The way we "approve what is excellent" is to encourage one another to engage in love and good deeds, as the Bible says in Hebrews 10:24. When we are giving our best for Christ and are urging and helping each other to do the same, we will produce "the fruit of righteousness."

There's a lot of conversation today about improving people's relationships. We get all kinds of advice. We certainly should seek godly counsel when it is needed, but to be truly fit for life, we must begin by putting first things first, living for what matters most. The purpose of the Christian life is to become more and more like Jesus Christ. When we are relating properly to Him and growing in His love, then our other relationships in life will become strong and healthy.

CHAPTER TWO

Totally Alive

Former Beatle John Lennon proclaimed in song that "life is what happens to you while you're making other plans." Lennon was killed at the untimely age of forty by a deranged fan in New York, and I can't help but wonder if Lennon ever considered the fact that death too happens to you while you're making other plans.

Of course, John Lennon was referring to the way so many people miss the most important moments of life because their minds are somewhere else. They're like the dad who is working excessively to provide for his son's future but misses the chance to eat dinner at night with his family or toss a ball with his son while the little guy still wants Dad to play catch with him.

Most people have made some kind of plans for life, and some have made financial plans for their death. But beyond your career or your next vacation or your family's future, what is your plan for life? Can you honestly say, "For to me to live is Christ, and to die is gain" (Philippians 1:21)? It's true that you're not ready to live until you're ready to die, and the exciting thing about the Christian life is that whether it involves life or death, God has a fantastic plan for your life. The details of that plan are as unique as you are, but the bottom line is that you will never really live until you are living for the Lord Jesus Christ. So how do you become totally alive?

YOU MUST EXPECT THAT GOD HAS A PERFECT PLAN FOR YOUR LIFE

Those who have grown up in the church have heard all of their lives that God has a wonderful plan for us—and it's true! The problem is, we've lived long enough to discover that while God's plan may be perfect, life is far from it. But please don't let the disappointments and defeats of life keep you from believing and knowing that God's plan for you really *is* perfect. It is orchestrated by the One who sees and knows everything, who never fails or makes a mistake, and who loves you with perfect love. As a matter of fact, the plan God has ordained for the lives of His children is so perfect that it can take even the imperfections and interruptions of our lives and work everything together for our eternal good and His eternal glory.

God's Plan for Your Life Is Centered in Jesus Christ

If you're hoping that I am about to give you ten easy steps or five foolproof secrets to finding God's plan for your life, you're going to be disappointed. What I do know is that there is only one "secret" to the Christian life, "To live is Christ." Once you get this, you will know what it means to be truly alive.

What gets you up every day? What gets you excited about life and enthusiastic about the day ahead of you? What is the purpose and the passion of your life? Can you say, "To me to live is Christ, and to die is gain"? Or are you still hoping you'll find something else or something more that will make life truly exciting and worth rolling out of bed for each morning?

Too many people are enduring instead of enjoying their lives. Their favorite day of the week is someday—someday they'll find that perfect relationship; someday they'll experience the blessing and fullness that other people seem to enjoy; someday they'll be happy; someday they'll get that promotion at work or build that dream home that will give them the fulfillment they seek.

Such persons fantasize about the future while enduring the present. Fulfillment is whatever they think will fulfill their lives out there somewhere. An astounding 94 percent of the people who responded to a survey said they were enduring the present while waiting for something better to happen in the future. Isn't it about time that you make every day matter?

The problem is that this imagined future never seems to arrive. Meanwhile, life goes on and years go by and so does life. Baseball great Mickey Mantle once said, "If I had known I was going to live this long, I'd have taken better care of myself." The gift of life is too valuable to waste.

So many people live their entire lives getting ready for that big moment that either never comes or passes them by while they're waiting for it. If this describes you, I have great news. God wants you to be fully and totally alive starting *today*, not someday.

Philippians 1:21 is a life-changing verse. Jesus is the source and secret of our lives. This is true because Jesus gave us life through His death for our sins on the cross and through His resurrection. Jesus is also the source of our strength each day. Only Jesus can give us the joy, peace, and purpose that God's Word promises to us. This is what Paul meant when he said that the secret to his life was Christ. When you know Jesus and you are drawing your strength and joy from Him each day, you are totally alive. Jesus will add years to your life and life to your years.

One reason Paul's words resonate with truth is that he had no earthly reason to write a book so full of joyful living as Philippians. Remember that he wrote Philippians not from a palace or even a pulpit but from a prison. He said in 1:12–13:

> *I want you to know, brothers, that what has happened to me has really served to advance the gospel, so that it has become known throughout the whole imperial guard and to all the rest that my imprisonment is for Christ.*

What an amazing statement. I'm afraid many people would stop short of saying they wanted Christ to be their life if they knew that it included a stint in prison. But Paul said his prison experience was for the sake of Christ. And he didn't turn bitter even when he discovered that some believers in Philippi were trying to undermine his ministry and challenge his credentials (1:15–17).

Paul considered his critics and concluded, "What then? Only that in every way, whether in pretense or in truth, Christ is proclaimed, and in that I rejoice. Yes, and I will rejoice" (v. 18). This man refused to allow anyone or anything to destroy his joy in Jesus.

You can't stop a person like that! Paul refused to quit on life. He refused to be beaten down by bitterness or defeated by disappointment or discouragement. Paul was a missionary who was constantly on the move because he wanted to take the gospel to the entire world—all the way to Caesar in Rome. Paul wanted to go to Rome as a preacher, but he ended up going as a prisoner. That was fine with him, as long as he could preach Christ all along the way and when he got to Rome. Paul had been badly beaten on his first trip to Philippi (Acts 16:22–23), and he had also been broken in body by other beatings and hardships. Yet his joyous spirit shines through in Philippians because Paul realized that his sufferings were not in vain. On the contrary, he told the Corinthians: "*For the sake of Christ*, then, I am content with weaknesses, insults, hardships, persecutions, and calamities. For when I am weak, then I am strong" (2 Corinthians 12:10, emphasis added). Paul wasn't a masochist who enjoyed pain. He was a Christian who was deeply committed to Christ and understood that quitting is never an option because Jesus is Lord of Life.

God Wants You to Learn That You Are Dependent on Him

Paul could say that he chose joy even in his trials because he had learned something. Before his conversion, Paul was a proud religious professional who despised the followers of Jesus (Philippians 3:5; Acts 9:1–2). He literally led a death squad that captured and killed Christians. In fact, I would call him a terrorist.

But something began to change in this rabid rabbi's brilliant but distorted mind. It probably began the day he held the garments of those who were stoning Stephen, the godly deacon and first martyr of the church (Acts 7:58). Paul, then known as Saul, enthusiastically approved of Stephen's death (Acts 8:1)

As he died, Stephen's face shone like the face of an angel. His face radiated with the love and forgiveness of Christ, and something began to stir in Saul's heart. Then on his way to Damascus, he met the risen

Redeemer (Acts 9). He came face to face with Jesus Christ, and Jesus transformed his life. It was then that this dangerous, arrogant, young rabbi discovered that without Christ he was totally and spiritually dead. Like many people, he was living a lifeless life. He desperately needed Jesus to change him and radically save him from his sin and its consequences. One way Jesus taught Paul this lesson was by blinding him for three days after his conversion, so that he became dependent on others to lead him around. But it was in his human weakness that Paul found his true strength.

This is the ultimate extreme makeover. It isn't just an external makeover; it is internal because salvation is an inside job. Saul became Paul, and the murderer became a missionary. Now here he was many years later in jail, still passionate about the fulfillment of God's plan in his life and rejoicing because even the terrible things that had happened to him were helping to advance the gospel and magnify Christ.

This man was joyous in every circumstance, faithful in his witness, and courageous in the face of death. That's the kind of life I want to live. That's the Christ life in us, and that's the definition of being totally alive.

It's critical that you not allow the disappointments and the defeats of life to destroy your faith. Life is too short to spend your days on hold waiting to live, wanting to live, but never truly living—or even worse, living in defeat.

I know bad things have happened to you because bad things happen to everybody. Maybe your career has been a disappointment, or your marriage is struggling. It could be that your health is failing, or you're wondering why God didn't answer your prayers. Life doesn't always turn out the way we prayed and planned, and disappointments can leave us feeling as if we're in a prison of pain or captives of problems that won't go away.

But the message of Scripture is that if you are a child of God, your pain isn't pointless. It has a purpose, which is that Jesus Christ will be magnified through your life. Just before he said, "to live is Christ," Paul wrote, "as it is my eager expectation and hope that I will not be at all ashamed, but that with full courage now as always Christ will be honored in my body, whether by life or by death" (Philippians 1:20).

Notice how completely Paul covered every eventuality in that bold statement. He said he didn't want to be ashamed in any way or by anything, and he wanted Christ to be exalted or magnified in his life "always," which pretty well covers it. And then he added, "whether by life or by death" just for good measure. What I'm saying is that Paul looked for God's hand and God's plan in everything. So how did Paul's imprisonment advance the purposes of the gospel?

Paul's Prison Became His Study

For one thing, Paul's prison time slowed him down long enough to write the book of Philippians and three other key epistles—Philemon, Ephesians, and Colossians. Read these prison epistles of Paul, and you'll see that they contain the heart of Christian teaching. It's hard to imagine being all that God wants us to be without the truths found in those books. Paul was such a high-energy man that he may not have turned aside to write these letters if he had not been on his forced "sabbatical" as a prisoner of Rome.

Paul's Prison Became His Pulpit

Another purpose of Paul's prison time was the opportunities it gave him to tell others about Christ. Paul didn't isolate himself from others or turn inward just because he was suffering unjustly. There was at least one Roman guard shackled to Paul at all times, and they changed shifts every six hours. I can hear the guard going off duty saying to the new guy coming on, "You'd better get ready because all this guy talks about is Jesus." Jesus was the theme and the subject of Paul's life, and he couldn't stop talking about his Lord.

All of us struggle in life. All of us are going to be knocked down from time to time, but we don't have to stay down. You're only a failure if you stay down when you fall. Being totally alive doesn't mean that you are never broken or never face setbacks. It means allowing God to work in those very areas where you feel the weakest so that you emerge stronger in the broken places.

That's not to say it's easy. Paul was broken in body not for doing the wrong thing, but for doing the right thing. As I said earlier, don't get the idea that he enjoyed pain. But we do know that he prayed and sang praises to God at Philippi with his feet in stocks and his back bleeding from a terrible beating. And because he and Silas were able to see and praise Jesus in their pain, a jailer and his family were saved.

God's Will Is for You to Say, "To Live Is Christ"

I hope you're realizing by now that being able to say, "For to me to live is Christ" has nothing to do with your circumstances. Even if you feel like you're on the bottom right now, lift up your eyes to Jesus Christ. Don't throw a pity party, because that's one party no one wants to attend. Life is too short to live it in bitterness and defeat, just trudging through each day trying to get to tomorrow, complaining and cursing the darkness.

Maybe you're saying, "This sounds good, but I've lost so much." You can't do anything about what is lost, but you can do something in Jesus' name with what's left! You can get up from defeat and heartache and begin again. There's a lot of living to be done if you will truly say, "God, here's my life. Take it and fill it with Jesus."

A POWERFUL TESTIMONY FROM SOMEONE WHO IS TOTALLY ALIVE

I want to close this chapter with an unusual testimony from a man who knows what power and success and fame are all about. His name is Ron Waterman, a former professional wrestler and mixed martial arts champion who was also a football star in school. Ron is the epitome of physical fitness and mental toughness. But something happened to Ron that changed him and made him fit for life in ways he never imagined.

※　※　※　※　※

I have had some amazing opportunities in my life. I was able to live out one of my childhood dreams while traveling around the world wrestling in the World Wrestling Federation against many of the guys I grew up watching on television. I was able to compete in the sport of mixed martial arts around the world with some of the toughest men on the planet. And a few years ago I was even fortunate enough to be included as a character in a video game.

But I also figured out a long time ago that none of those things—money, power, and fame—can buy your happiness. They can't buy your soul, and they certainly won't buy you an eternity in heaven. I'd like to tell you how I learned that.

My life wasn't always full of success and accomplishments.

When I was twelve years old, my parents divorced. I'd spend a weekend with Mom and then a weekend with Dad, much like many kids do today. My parents would try to make these weekends real special, but I grew up very prideful and independent. I blamed myself for their divorce, which I think is a common thing with young kids when their parents split up.

I bottled up all of my anger and turned to athletics to try to find my self-worth. I ended up being fairly successful on the football field and on the wrestling mat. I worked hard enough to earn myself a college scholarship. I wrestled in college, which is where I met my wife, during my first year. She was on a track and field scholarship; so it seemed that we had many things in common. We both loved sports and the outdoors, and we both loved children.

One of the things we thought we had in common was our belief that we knew who God was. We simply thought that if that day were to come in our lives when we were to stand in front of God Almighty, we would certainly be let into heaven because we were good people. We compared ourselves to our friends and thought that if we lived a cleaner life than they did, we would make it into heaven.

Well, we ended up getting married, had two beautiful sons, graduated from college, and took off with successful careers. But the problem was that my wife's career took her in one direction while my career took me in a different direction. The result was that after eleven years of marriage, we felt ourselves holding on to our marriage by a thread.

About the only thing we had in common after those eleven years were two small boys who needed their mom and dad to be together. But you see, when you're out there living for the world, for money, for possessions, and for all of the excitement, you can only do that for so long. Sooner or later the world is going to catch up to you.

I remember coming home from work one night and thumbing through the Yellow Pages, looking for a divorce attorney. I saw no other solution. The problems that had built up in our lives and marriage were so great, I didn't see any way we were going to make it through. We had tried counseling and all the things the world had to offer, but the problems just seemed to pile up and get bigger and bigger. I saw myself heading down the path my parents took when I was twelve years old.

One Sunday morning my father called and invited us to go to church with him. He'd invited us many times before, but we would turn him down. We were far too busy to take two hours out of our schedule to go to church. But we figured at this point, what did we have to lose? So my wife and I agreed to go.

As we sat in church with my father that Sunday morning, I was certain that someone had tipped off that pastor before I arrived, because I felt every word out of his mouth was directed right at me. As he stood up there and spoke, his words pierced through my skin and grabbed hold of my heart. Something was happening inside of me that day that I couldn't explain and had never felt before, but it was all I could do to hold back the tears. When I looked beside me, hoping my wife was feeling what I felt inside, tears began to flow down her face, and I knew that she was feeling the same thing I felt.

It was just a short time after this that we returned to that church, walked down the middle aisle, knelt at the altar, and asked Jesus Christ to come into our lives, to be our Lord and Savior. I can't tell you how many ways my life has changed since that day. The problems that were so overwhelming in our lives, that I thought there was no solution to, God dealt with one at a time.

One of my favorite Scriptures is John 10:10, where Jesus said, "The thief comes only to steal and kill and destroy." As I look back at my life, Satan was so close to stealing, killing, and destroying everything I held close to my heart, everything I loved, everything I cherished. He was so close to taking my two boys and my wife. But the second part of that verse is what I like so well: "I came that they may have life and have it abundantly."

There's one thing that brings me to my knees every single day of my life, and that is God's grace. The fact that He was still willing to come into my life after thirty-two years of all my bad choices and all my mistakes, that He was still willing to walk up to me, hold out His hand, and take thirty-two years of garbage off my back and put it on His own—do we have an awesome God or what!

I can't say that ever since that day my wife and I haven't had one disagreement. You know better, because we live in a real world and we're going to face challenges and obstacles every day. But now instead of bottling up our problems and running off in different directions, we come together, put our hands together, and look up, because Jesus Christ is the only One with answers.

✳ ✳ ✳ ✳ ✳

Needless to say, the testimony of what it took to bring a powerful and proud man like Ron Waterman to his knees is electrifying. I share it with you in the hope that if you are at the end of yourself and fresh out of answers, if your marriage is barely hanging on, or if you're facing problems so great that you can't deal with them, you will do what Ron did and bow at the feet of Jesus. No matter what damage has been done in a life or a marriage, God can make a way where there seems to be no way.

And even if you're flying high right now and feel on top of the world, the day will come when you land. And if you don't know Jesus Christ, it won't matter what else you have because nothing can keep you from landing hard and crashing except the love and grace of God that Ron Waterman described so well.

A successful, middle-aged woman in the Midwest recently put almost all of her possessions up for auction online on eBay. She was asked by an interviewer on a national radio program why she was selling everything except some personal papers and family heirloom antiques, which she was donating to a historical museum. This woman explained that she wanted to be happy and realized that she had allowed comfort to replace adventure and meaning in her life. So she was moving to a different part of the country, and her goal was to have fewer things but a larger life.

I don't know that woman's spiritual condition, but her discovery that things don't equal happiness is one step on the road to discovering how to be totally alive. Of course, real life is found only in Jesus Christ, and I pray that if you haven't yet trusted Him as your Savior, or if you've allowed other things to crowd into your life, you will renew your commitment to live for Christ, and for Christ alone.

CHAPTER THREE

Far Better

One thing that many people quickly discover when they start a fitness program is that doing repeated exercises or jogging on a treadmill can be boring. A lot of people bring their own entertainment with them, but most health clubs also have a bank of televisions installed above their treadmills so people can watch the news while they get in shape. I've often wondered if someone huffing and puffing on a treadmill ever listened to the reports about fanatic world leaders with nuclear capabilities and all the other terrible things going on in our world and said to himself, *Why am I bothering to get in shape?*

That's a question I'm not here to answer, but there is one feature of those televisions in health clubs that I find interesting. They cause the viewer to look up as he or she works to get fit. I think the apostle Paul for one would approve of that idea, because he was always looking up and calling God's people to do the same. We've heard the old saying about people who are so heavenly minded they're no earthly good. But the Bible teaches that we are really no earthly good *until* we are heavenly minded.

Paul was so heavenly minded that he revealed to the Philippians his intense longing and desire to leave this earth and go to be with Christ. After stating the great purpose of his life in Philippians 1:21, "For to me to live is Christ, and to die is gain," Paul continued by saying, "If I am to live in the flesh, that means fruitful labor for me. Yet which I shall choose I cannot tell. I am hard pressed between the two. My desire is to depart and be with Christ, *for that is far better*" (vv. 22–23, emphasis added).

THERE IS NO HIGHER DESIRE FOR THE CHRISTIAN THAN THE DESIRE FOR HEAVEN

Paul used a strong superlative form here that means "far, far, far better." For him, it did not get any better than going home to heaven and being in the presence of Jesus. Heaven is the promise of God for His people, and it ought to be every Christian's passion to know Christ, to live for Christ, and then to be with Christ forever. Paul was looking forward to heaven.

In fact, Paul said he had a problem because he really wanted to go to heaven right then. But he also knew that the church at Philippi and the other churches he had established throughout the first-century world needed his leadership as an apostle. Already false teachers had begun to circle the flock of believers like a pack of wolves, and Paul was deeply concerned about the maturity and stability of his spiritual children. But nevertheless, his heart longed for home.

Heaven Is a Win-Win Situation for God's People

As far as Paul could see, he was in a win-win situation. If he went to heaven he would see Jesus, and if he stayed on earth he would be able to plant and reap more spiritual fruit. That's why he could say in essence, "If I live I win, because I live for Christ. And if I die I win too, because I go to be with Him in glory, which is far, far better."

As Christians we need to remind ourselves that the best is yet to come. If you know Christ, you have a guaranteed future with Him forever. I don't know of anything that will destroy people's hope, motivation, or passion for living faster than the belief that their best days are behind them—that whatever it was that made their life meaningful and gave them significance is over and all they have left now is waiting for the end to come.

One of the saddest examples of this was H. L. Mencken, a famous journalist in the first half of the twentieth century. Mencken was a brilliant wit and thinker until he suffered a stroke in 1948 that crippled his mental faculties. Seven years later, a man who visited Mencken was talking with him about a mutual friend who had passed away in 1948. When he heard the year of his friend's death mentioned, Mencken replied, "That's right, I believe he died the year I did."

Here was a man who had lived for seven years feeling as if he were already dead. What a contrast to the joyful anticipation with which we are called to approach the issues of life and death. Of course, our bodies and minds can suffer debilitating diseases. But despite it all, we can live with joy because we know this life isn't all there is. It's not even the end, because we have something far, far better ahead of us.

When you can truly say you are ready and willing to go and see Christ or to stay where He has placed you for as long as He wants you there, you've moved a long way toward being fit for life. I'd have to say most aren't quite at that point yet. They want to go to heaven; they just don't want to die to get there. They're like the old man who was asked what he wanted said about him at his funeral. He thought for a minute and replied, "Look, he's moving!" We often want to keep moving because we are not really convinced that heaven is far, far better than anything here on earth. But the fact is, we are on our way to the ultimate victory of the life of faith, which will come when we see Jesus face to face.

Death Should Hold No Fear for the Believer in Christ

One of the ironies of the Christian life is that you have to die in order to live. We must die to sin and self before we can be alive to Christ. But the great thing is that once we are alive in Christ, death can no longer dominate us. The Bible says in 1 Corinthians 15:54 that the moment we leave this world and go to be with Christ, "Death is swallowed up in victory." Then he asked and answered these questions: "'O death, where is your victory? O death, where is your sting?' The sting of death is sin, and the power of sin is the law. But thanks be to God, who gives us the victory through our Lord Jesus Christ" (vv. 55–57).

This means that death holds no power over or terror for the Christian. Death's power has been broken because God took the judgment of our sin and placed it on Christ at the cross. But it gets even better, because knowing Christ also takes away the fear of death. Many sincere Christians would say they know that death is simply moving from earth to heaven, but they're still afraid at the thought of dying.

Let me remind you that the Scriptures say that Jesus took on humanity to die for us, so that by His death "he might destroy the one who has the power of death, that is, the devil, and deliver all those who through fear of death were subject to lifelong slavery" (Hebrews 2:14–15). Death is described as a shadow in God's Word because a shadow has no power to hurt you. A shadow can frighten you, but it can never really harm you. So when we walk through the valley of the shadow of death we fear no evil for the presence of God is with us (Psalm 23:4).

Now let me ask you something. If heaven is far better than anything we could possibly have on earth, and if we have no reason to fear the pathway (death) by which we enter heaven, what can keep us from living an abundant life here on earth while looking forward to heaven? Nothing! Life is too short to just trudge through it with our heads down, feeling defeated and depressed. Let's live looking up in faith.

We are to live with our hearts in heaven. "If then you have been raised with Christ, seek the things that are above, where Christ is, seated at the right hand of God. Set your minds on things that are above, not on things that are on earth" (Colossians 3:1–2).

We are already seated with Christ in heaven (Ephesians 2:6), so why shouldn't our focus be there now? The word translated "minds" has the idea of affections, the things that motivate and move us at the deepest level of our being. This is not an option—it is a command. It's when we set our hearts on heaven that we are able to live with confidence and certainty. Spend your life seeking heaven and expecting a great life now and forever.

THE DESIRE FOR HEAVEN IS MORE THAN JUST AN EXIT STRATEGY FROM LIFE

Please don't get the idea that Paul wanted to escape life.

I don't want you to get the idea that Paul said he was ready to go and be with Christ because he was so tired of life with its pain and prison and struggles that he just wanted to escape it all. He was not looking for an exit strategy to get himself out of a tough situation as painlessly and quickly as possible.

Determine to Live for Christ Every Day You're Alive

That wasn't Paul's attitude at all. He was loving his life in Christ and was excited about sharing Christ with people throughout the world of his day. When I talk about living for the "far better" future awaiting us in heaven, I'm not suggesting that we ought to be looking to check out as soon as possible. We ought to take care of ourselves physically and emotionally and live as long as we can.

Remember that Paul's goal was to magnify Christ "in my body" (Philippians 1:20). Our bodies are meant to glorify God because we are the temple of the Holy Spirit (1 Corinthians 6:19). We are to discipline our bodies like an athlete running to win the prize (1 Corinthians 9:24–27). We only have one body, and we are to maintain our physical fitness so we can live our best for God's glory. So live your life fully. Enjoy every day. Take good care of your health. Make a difference in the world for the sake of the Kingdom. Never give up on life until Jesus comes to take you home to be with Him.

Accept the Testimony of Someone Who Saw the Glories of Heaven

Another aspect of our longing for heaven is also relevant. As far as we know, Paul was the only person who ever got to visit heaven while he was still alive and come back to talk about it. He described that incredible experience in 2 Corinthians 12:2 as being "caught up to the third heaven," the dwelling place of God. He called this place "paradise" (v. 3). During this vision, Paul said, he saw and heard things that he couldn't talk about. All he could say was that he was overwhelmed by "the surpassing greatness of the revelations" (v. 7).

We can only imagine what he saw. Whatever those indescribable sights and sounds were, after that experience he was never the same. Paul might say that if we knew how wonderful and how glorious heaven really is, we would live every day with a new perspective.

An incredible future is waiting for everyone who knows Christ— you and me included. That's what's so encouraging about this testimony from a man who went to heaven and lived to tell about it! This isn't someone telling you about his vacation. This is a friend saying, "Just wait until you get there too and see what I saw!" That changes everything. By faith we can be excited about heaven. By faith we can live with this hope and sure confidence that heaven really is "far, far better."

Realize That the Glories of Heaven Far Outweigh the Sufferings of Earth

This mind-boggling report on heaven is reliable because it is described in God's inerrant Word. Since Paul saw heaven, we can also believe him when he said, "I consider that the sufferings of this present time are not worth comparing with the glory that is to be revealed to us" (Romans 8:18). Here's a person who suffered as few other believers have ever suffered and saw the joys of heaven in a way no other believer has ever seen them, and he says the sufferings are nothing compared to the glory.

We can conclude that the problems and perplexities of life now are "momentary" (2 Corinthians 4:17), while the pleasures of the next life are eternal. The psalmist said, "In your presence there is fullness of joy; at your right hand are pleasures forevermore" (Psalm 16:11). Here's the perspective we need: "We look not to the things that are seen but to the things that are unseen. For the things that are seen are transient, but the things that are unseen are eternal" (2 Corinthians 4:18). Once you embrace this reality, you're ready to embrace life.

THE BEST DAY YOU WILL EVER HAVE IS STILL AHEAD OF YOU

The best day you will ever have will be the day that you step into heaven and see Jesus face to face. That means your best life is still ahead of you. Entering heaven is not leaving home—it's *going home*.

We Should Have an Insatiable Hunger for Heaven

A word in Philippians 1:23 gives us a sense of just how we are to long for heaven. Paul said, "My desire is to depart and be with Christ." The word translated "desire" is very strong. It's an intensified form of the word used elsewhere in Scripture for "lust" (see 1 John 2:16, KJV). This may surprise you. Paul had a holy lust—an insatiable, God-given desire—for heaven. He was heaven-hearted.

If we have a holy lust for the right things, we won't be controlled by unholy lusts for the wrong things. We don't usually associate lust with holiness, but when our God-given desires are channeled in the right direction, they can have a purifying effect on us. "And everyone who thus hopes in him [Christ] purifies himself" (1 John 3:3). Heaven is our holy ambition.

I want you to see the full impact of another word that Paul used in Philippians 1:23 to help us understand why our best day will be the day we enter heaven. This is the word "depart," which the great apostle used to describe the moment he would trade earth for heaven. This word was used in a number of ways in the ancient world, and when we put them together we have a beautiful word picture of what it means for the Christian to leave earth and go to heaven. For example, this word was often used to describe a soldier striking his tent and marching home in victory.

Tents were a common form of housing in Paul's world, and he in fact was a tentmaker by trade. So it's not surprising that he used the imagery of folding up a tent to describe the moment when we lay aside these temporary earthly bodies and depart for heaven: "For we know that if the tent that is our earthly home is destroyed, we have a building from God, a house not made with hands, eternal in the heavens" (2 Corinthians 5:1).

This is a reference to the new, perfect, eternal bodies we will receive in heaven. And not only will we have new bodies, we'll have a new home to put them in. The night before Jesus' crucifixion, He told His disciples, "In my Father's house are many rooms. If it were not so, would I have told you that I go to prepare a place for you?" (John 14:2). The word "rooms" is translated as "mansions" in the *King James Version.*

I don't know about you, but my earthly "tent" is getting a little frayed around the edges. I have a few flaps hanging out on my tent, and the weather's beating it down a little bit. But I'm looking forward to the day when I fold it up and march home in victory.

For many months after Hurricane Katrina devastated our Gulf Coast, tens of thousands of victims were still living in tents. Others who were able to leave their tents behind and move into an apartment or other permanent dwelling talked about their absolute elation at having electricity, running water, plumbing, and other necessities we take for granted. When we go to heaven, we will not only survive life's storms, but we will live in a place more wonderful than our minds can imagine.

The word translated "depart" in Philippians 1:23 was also used to describe sailors pulling up the anchor of a ship and setting sail for distant shores. When we see a ship sail into the distance and disappear on the horizon, we say, "She's gone." But the ship isn't gone, of course. It's just beyond our sight.

Sometimes we stand by the grave of a loved one and say that person is "gone." But they're not gone—they're just out of our sight. The truth is that believers who have departed for heaven are more alive in the presence of Christ than they ever were here on earth. That's why Paul said heaven is far better.

Can you imagine being completely free of all our limitations and pain and sailing high, wide, and handsome in the presence of God forever? Sailors talk about the feeling of freedom on the open seas. But when we set sail for heaven, we'll experience a freedom that's beyond comprehension.

A third way that the word translated "depart" was used in ancient times was to describe the unraveling of a problem. The picture is that of a complicated knot that is finally untied. Have you ever had a knot in your brain, a problem you just couldn't figure out or unravel? And when the answer finally came, you felt such a sense of discovery and satisfaction. That's what heaven is going to be like.

There are questions about life that we will never understand this side of heaven. When the awful massacre at Virginia Tech occurred in 2007, people wanted to know why, but one television commentator said, "We may never know why." He's right. Life is filled with unsolvable problems.

Read these words about what we know now and what we will know then: "For we know in part and we prophesy in part, but when the perfect comes, the partial will pass away" (1 Corinthians 13:9–10). Then he adds, "For now we see in a mirror dimly, but then face to face. Now I know in part; *then I shall know fully*, even as I have been fully known" (v. 12, emphasis added).

Someday we are going to "know fully," and we will keep knowing and growing because heaven is going to be a wonderful place of discovery of who God is and what He does. Heaven will be far better because we will move from questions to answers. It will all make perfect sense when we know fully what God was doing in our lives. When you see Christ, you will look at your life, all the good and bad, and it will make perfect sense. In heaven we will often hear "Oh, now I understand." Surely, as the old hymn says, "we will understand it better by and by."

One more picture is suggested by the word "depart" that I want you to see. This word was used of a farmer who would take the yoke off his oxen after a long day of hard work and let them rest. Heaven is a place of eternal rest. Whatever burden or load you are carrying, I want you to know that in heaven you will move from suffering and hard work to perfect peace. Remember how good it feels to put down a heavy load, and how light on your feet you feel when you are finally free of the burden? That's a picture of the rest waiting for us in heaven when we depart to be with Christ.

Enjoy Each Day to the Full, Knowing That It Will Get Even Better Later

We've looked at some great examples of the "far betterness" of heaven. But I also love the balance struck in the following verses of Philippians 1 in relation to this matter of going to heaven or staying behind: "To remain in the flesh is more necessary on your account. Convinced of this, I know that I will remain and continue with you all, for your progress and joy in the faith" (vv. 24–25).

Paul wasn't complaining about staying behind. We've already seen that Paul was so heavenly minded and heaven-hearted that he was prepared to live each day in full joy and abandon to Jesus Christ. C. S. Lewis once said, "The Christians who did most for the present world were precisely those who thought most of the next."

A godly man was dying while his son stood next to his bed. Knowing that his father was about to enter heaven, his son asked, "Dad, how do you feel?"

His dad looked up, smiled, and said, "Like a little boy on Christmas Eve."

I want to live each day to the maximum, being in the best state of spiritual, physical, mental, and emotional fitness I can possibly achieve. But I also never want to lose sight of something ahead that is far better than anything I can comprehend. I've had some great moments and days in my life, and I hope you have as well. But the best day we will ever have is the day when we meet Christ in heaven.

CHAPTER FOUR

Honoring God with Our Bodies

Being fit for life includes taking care of the bodies God has given us. But apparently so many people today are living unhealthy and over-stressed lives that they've come up with a new term in the workforce: *presenteeism*. As opposed to absenteeism, presenteeism describes people who show up at work but who are so fatigued and unhealthy that they are unable to put in a full day's work, and so workplace productivity suffers. It goes without saying that people who are sluggish and unproductive at work are also not likely contributing fully to their families or churches either. This is one reason that any study of fitness from a biblical perspective must include the physical side of spirituality.

There is really no way to separate the physical and spiritual components of our human makeup because they are so intricately related. Whoever thinks being spiritual allows us to ignore the physical hasn't read God's Word very carefully. Paul's prayer for the believers at Thessalonica gives us a big clue to the importance God places on our bodies: "Now may the God of peace himself sanctify you completely, and may your whole spirit and soul and body be kept blameless at the coming of our Lord Jesus Christ" (1 Thessalonians 5:23). I like the way this reads in *The Message*: "May God himself, the God who makes everything holy and whole, make you holy and whole, put you together—spirit, soul, and body—and keep you fit for the coming of our

Master, Jesus Christ. The One who called you is completely dependable. If he said it, he'll do it!"

The Christian is body, soul, and spirit, and it is the balance of life that matters most. Dr. Adrian Rogers said, "With our spirits, we have spiritual life and relate to the world above us; with our souls, we have emotional life and relate to the world within us; and with our bodies we have physical life and relate to the world around us. When we're right spiritually, we're holy, when we're right emotionally, we're happy, and when we're right physically, we're healthy."

That's a great summary of the way we can be sanctified, which is the process by which we grow to be more like Jesus Christ. It's clear that God's will for our sanctification includes our bodies. In fact, without this our sanctification would be incomplete. Paul's prayer also indicates that God's desire and will for us is that we be as blameless in body as we are in our spirits and souls.

Paul expressed his desire to be at his best physically in Philippians 1:20, which I want to reference again: "It is my eager expectation and hope that I will not be at all ashamed, but that with full courage now as always Christ will be honored in my body." Paul was determined that if God chose to leave him on earth for the sake of the church, he was going to finish his course with energy.

This is the physical side of being spiritual. To take care of our bodies, to honor God with our bodies, is both biblical and practical. Some Greek philosophers of Paul's day taught that the spirit is good while the body is evil, but the Bible refutes that false dichotomy because, as we read above, God wants our bodies to be sanctified. The apostle John wrote, "I pray that all may go well with you and that you may be in good health, as it goes well with your soul" (3 John 2). For as long as we live, we ought to be vital in our faith and in our fitness. To do less would mean being ashamed before Christ or bringing shame to the name of Christ, and Paul said that was the last thing he wanted to do.

CHRIST IS OUR PERFECT EXAMPLE OF PHYSICAL WHOLENESS

One of the most profound mysteries of our faith is that God became man. The writer of Hebrews said, "When Christ came into the world, he said, 'Sacrifices and offerings you have not desired, but a body have you prepared for me'" (10:5). When God sent His Son to live in a human body, the body was elevated to a new level of dignity and importance.

Jesus Himself was no doubt physically fit. He traveled extensively and walked everywhere He went. Anyone who has been to Israel and has seen the rugged terrain from Galilee to Jerusalem can appreciate how physically strong and fit Jesus had to be just to carry out His ministry. Don't think of Jesus as being a pale, emaciated, sanctimonious recluse as He is depicted in some medieval paintings. He was a man's man who carried the cross and the weight of the world on His shoulders.

Luke 2:52 provides an insight into the way Jesus grew and developed while on earth: "Jesus increased in wisdom and in stature and in favor with God and man." The Lord grew intellectually, physically, spiritually, and socially as He enjoyed the favor of God and the people around Him. Jesus is the perfect example of what it means to be fit for life.

And just as Jesus our example offered His body as a sacrifice on the cross, so we are to "present [our] bodies as a living sacrifice, holy and acceptable to God" (Romans 12:1). In other words, our calling is to give God our best, which is hard to do if we're in poor physical condition.

What is involved in living full and fulfilling lives in terms of caring for our bodies, with the goal of honoring Christ? Here are some principles from Scripture that have to do with how to treat our bodies so we can be at our best for the Lord.

TREAT YOUR BODY WITH HONOR AND REVERENCE AS THE TEMPLE OF GOD

The reason Paul could say he wanted to honor Christ in his body and could call us to offer our bodies to God as an act of worship is because of the truth he recorded in 1 Corinthians 6:19–20: "Do you not know that your body is a temple of the Holy Spirit within you, whom you have from God? You are not your own, for you were bought with a price. So glorify God in your body." The Christian's body is a holy vessel, set apart for the Lord. If you neglect or abuse your body, you limit yourself in your ability to glorify and magnify Him.

There is no higher honor God could give to our bodies than to call them His temple. His Word also dignifies and elevates the body by using it as an illustration of His church (1 Corinthians 12:12–31). Perhaps the most commonly used metaphor for the church today is "the body of Christ," the visible expression of Christ on earth.

Scripture leaves no doubt about how seriously God takes His temple. Speaking in the plural to the church, Paul said, "Do you not know that you are God's temple and that God's Spirit dwells in you? If anyone destroys God's temple, God will destroy him. For God's temple is holy, and you are that temple" (1 Corinthians 3:16–17). By analogy we could say that God holds us to an equally high standard in the use of our physical bodies.

It Matters to God What We Put on Our Bodies

The Bible speaks about how we are to dress the body and appear before others. The biblical principle is modesty, as Paul explained: "Women should adorn themselves in respectable apparel, with modesty and self-control, not with braided hair and gold or pearls or costly attire, but with what is proper for women who profess godliness—with good works" (1 Timothy 2:9–10).

That is, women are to dress in clothing that reflects a modest or chaste attitude toward their bodies, thus honoring God. To wear clothes that are provocative and promote sensuality or sexuality does not honor the body, nor does it honor God, but dishonors and disgraces His temple.

This attitude is radically counter to the culture we live in, which is why we have to take our cues from the Word and not from the world. Modesty begins not in our wardrobe but in our hearts. A man or woman who dresses to allure or impress others instead of to reflect the character of Christ has lost sight of this all-encompassing principle: "Whatever you do, do all to the glory of God" (1 Corinthians 10:31). This doesn't mean a woman or young girl has to dress like a spinster. But a person can be beautiful without being immodest.

The question is, whom are we trying to please by what we wear? Both men and women who profess to know Christ are to honor Him by what they put on their bodies, and I see it as the responsibility of the church to be an environment in which modesty and purity are affirmed, appreciated, and welcomed. For whom are you dressing? As a Christian, your appearance should reflect the life of Christ who is in you.

It Matters to God What We Put in Our Bodies

An amazing exhibit called Body Worlds displays the work of a German physician who developed a technique to preserve parts of the body by injecting them with a substance he invented. This display features room after room of real human bodies with muscles, nerves, blood vessels, organs, bones, and every other imaginable body part preserved in intricate detail.

One of the exhibits showed a normal human lung and the lung of a smoker, blackened by tar deposits and disease. Beside it was a large display with a clear plastic box attached to the front and a small television screen set into it. The display urged people to quit smoking and encouraged them to drop their tobacco products into the box, then sign and take with them a card that said, "I quit" as a reminder of their pledge.

The screen featured a short message from the late actor Yul Brynner, recorded just before his death from lung cancer after being a two-pack-a-day smoker. Brynner said that if he had one message he could give to people, it would be, "Don't smoke. Just don't do it!" The overall impact of the display was quite powerful, and the clear plastic box was half full of cigarette packs and even matchbooks.

I applaud a message about tobacco that says, "Just don't do it!" Of course, as Christians we could expand that message to anything that damages our bodies, our testimony, and our effectiveness for Christ. "Just don't do it." But tobacco is a good place to start because these products are known killers.

Our nation was horrified by the rash of church burnings a few years ago as arsonists destroyed God's "temples." As far as I'm concerned, a smoking Christian is an arsonist who is destroying God's temple. It's just a lot slower, and it isn't against the law. If you're a smoker, I challenge you to sign a card or take a pledge or get whatever help and support you need to quit.

Regarding alcohol, I made a decision as a teenager to be a total abstainer because I was convinced from Scripture that using alcohol was not going to help me in my Christian walk. After more than thirty years as a pastor, seeing the damage that alcohol does to lives and families, I'm more convinced than ever that we need to abstain from alcohol.

Whenever the subject of abstinence from alcohol comes up, two objections are usually raised. First, someone will point out that the Bible does not explicitly forbid drinking alcoholic beverages. And second, someone will say, "I am very modest and temperate in my use of alcohol. I don't drink to excess." Or to put it more slangily, "I can handle my liquor."

It's true there is no verse in the Bible that says, "Thou shalt not drink." And modesty in drink is certainly better than indulgence. But that's not the end of the argument. Other principles from Scripture come into play, such as Romans 14:21: "It is good not to eat meat or drink wine or do anything that causes your brother to stumble."

We have a responsibility as Christians both to our Lord and to those around us. I always cringe when someone talks about their ability to handle alcohol because I want to ask, "What if your child doesn't have the same self-control? What if some other child, teen, or adult is watching and imitating you? Do you want to be responsible for introducing someone else to alcohol who *can't* 'handle it' and falls into abuse?" That's something I wouldn't want on my conscience.

I admire the decision made by a man named David Smith, who was a member of the Richard Childress racing team on the mega-popular NASCAR circuit. In a copyrighted article, "Leaving Over Liquor," that appeared in the *Charlotte Observer* on February 15, 2005, Smith said he decided to quit drinking alcoholic beverages for the sake of his Christian testimony and because as a former drinker he knows what alcohol does to people. Interestingly, the AMA is fighting NASCAR's ties with the liquor industry. The AMA said that with ten million underage American youth already drinking alcohol, and with alcohol involved in one-third of all car accidents that kill teenagers, advertising liquor on race cars is sending the wrong message.

You can make all the nuanced arguments you want about drinking alcohol, but the fact is that total abstinence doesn't kill people on the highway, doesn't cripple industry, doesn't destroy families, and doesn't undermine health or character or morals. And it is not contrary to the principle of love and compassion.

Well, these are the two "biggies," but I can't leave the subject of what we put in our bodies without addressing the issue of food. Dr. Howard Hendricks of Dallas Theological Seminary used to tell his students, "Overeating is the one acceptable sin in evangelical Christian circles." This man traveled extensively, and he said the problem was that everywhere he went, people fed him like it was his last meal. He gained so much weight that it became a real problem until he disciplined himself to get in good shape.

There is a national epidemic of obesity, including children. We're more aware of the health effects of what we eat than ever before, but disciplining ourselves to eat moderately is another story.

The "battle of the bulge" is a lifelong struggle for some people, but really it's no different than any other discipline of the Christian life that requires commitment and effort. And while it's true that I'd rather meet a fat man than a drunk on the highway, it's also possible to eat ourselves to death.

TREAT YOUR BODY WITH RESPECT BY THROWING AWAY NEGATIVE ATTITUDES

The book of Philippians really amazes me as I see the strong, positive, expectant attitude of a servant of Christ who was in terribly negative conditions. Paul's life was filled with "eager expectation and hope" (1:20) even though he was in prison. He was not consumed by all the negative attitudes and toxic emotions that so often drain our bodies and our lives of their vitality. So many Christians are stressed out because of life's pressures—or to be more candid, the pressures they put on themselves.

Negative emotions break down our physical system and drain us of energy. The writers of Scripture understood the connection between our minds and bodies long before modern psychiatry and psychology discovered it. This body-spirit connection is so powerful that your outlook in one area impacts you in every other area.

Since we're talking about the physical body here, let's consider the impact of attitudes on our health. One place where we can see this very clearly is in the relationship between our attitudes and our eating. Many people overeat when they are overly stressed or emotionally upset. Dr. Kenneth Cooper, among others, has pointed out that desserts spelled backwards is s-t-r-e-s-s-e-d.

Others drive their bodies to dangerous limits to achieve some goal, finish a big project at the office, or climb the next rung on the corporate ladder. Anger is a big motivator for some people, and the adrenaline it pumps into the system can enable a person to achieve some amazing things. But the long-term toll that attitudes such as anger take on us isn't worth the price.

That's why I believe the most important choice you and I make every day is the choice of our attitude, especially the first five or ten minutes after we get up in the morning.

We should always practice the truth of Psalm 118:24: "This is the day that the LORD has made; let us rejoice and be glad in it."

TREAT YOUR BODY WITH CARE BY TRAINING IT EACH DAY

First Corinthians 9:27 reads as clearly in the Greek as it does in English: "I discipline my body and keep it under control." That was Paul's testimony for himself and his challenge to us to stay physically fit.

We've talked about the importance of discipline in our eating and drinking. I'm talking to you as a fellow traveler. The problem is that once you reach a certain age, you stop growing on both ends and start growing in the middle. We need discipline! Unfortunately, there are plenty of establishments around town to help us fall off the wagon.

I have a friend whose church in Dallas was across the street from a doughnut shop. He said so many of his church's Sunday school classes had standing doughnut orders for Sunday morning, and so many individual members stopped in to eat, that they could have held church right there in the shop. He also said that when the church was going well, he couldn't tell whether they were having revival or were just on a sugar high.

We all know what we're talking about here. That's why we pray to lose weight, perhaps using this dieter's prayer:

Lord, grant me the strength that I might not fall
into the clutches of cholesterol,
and polyunsaturates I'll never mutter,
for the road to hell is paved with butter.
And cake is cursed, and cream is awful,
and Satan is hiding in every waffle.
Beelzebub is a chocolate drop;
Lucifer is a lollipop.
Teach me the evils of hollandaise,
of paste and globs of mayonnaise
and crisp fried chicken from the south.
Lord, if You love me, shut my mouth.

Let's be honest. Most of us are not going to live in deprivation. But we do need to learn the discipline and the freedom of moderation. Anyone who has battled indulgence in any area and has overcome it will tell you how freeing it is to be able to enjoy things in moderation. The irony of overindulgence is that the more you indulge in something, the less you enjoy it.

I hope I don't need to convince you of the importance of regular exercise. I mentioned how physically fit Jesus had to have been to travel on foot as much as He did and still have the strength to minister all day and sometimes half the night. People of earlier generations were probably more naturally fit than we are simply because they engaged in more physical labor.

Most people simply need to get moving. Walking is probably the oldest form of exercise in human history, and now we know that simple walking improves health and mental well-being. Our ancestors enjoyed the benefits of exercise without knowing all the physiology and psychology, while we know all the physiology and psychology but don't enjoy the benefits.

When I was a young seminarian in the early seventies, I picked up a book entitled *Aerobics*. It was written by a young Christian physician named Kenneth Cooper, and through that book Dr. Cooper had an enormous impact on my life as a college athlete and later in ministry. I never dreamed that one day I would be Ken Cooper's pastor or that he would be my personal physician. Today Ken is still a world-renowned leader in the area of health and fitness and is a shining example of what he teaches. I asked him to share some thoughts and a challenge on physical fitness and how it relates to faith:

*   *   *   *   *

I've been called "the father of aerobics" because I coined the term in 1966 and wrote the book *Aerobics* in 1968. I founded the Cooper Aerobic Center in Dallas and have been involved there over the past thirty-seven years. We've had over eighty thousand patients come to the Center—some one time and some every year since we've been open.

The Aerobic Center is a fitness center, but we have a spiritual dimension to our campus too. Bible studies are held throughout the week along with the physical exercise. We are told in Scripture to glorify God in our bodies as well as in our spirits. But a lot of us don't do that. Look at the obesity problem we have in America today. I'm convinced that you can't really enjoy life to the fullest and live a long, healthy life unless you adhere to the concept of regular conditioning and exercise and control your weight and your diet.

And combining that with spiritual fitness and daily prayer and Bible study will enable you to enjoy that very long, healthy, and full life. My goal is to live a long, healthy life to the fullest and then die suddenly. We call that squaring off the curve. What better goal and objective could we have than preparing ourselves for transition to heaven?

But we know that we are challenged to be physically fit because we are told to glorify God in our bodies. To do that I found that combining daily prayer and Bible study with regular conditioning, and watching my diet and my weight, gives me the best hope of living that long and healthy life.

How much time does it take to get spiritually and physically fit? In some thirty-seven years of research at our clinic, our studies show that getting at least thirty minutes of collective activity most days of the week, such as walking up and down stairs, can reduce deaths from all causes—heart attacks, strokes, diabetes, cancer, etc.—by 58 percent, which has the potential of increasing your life span for up to six years.

If you were to combine thirty minutes of physical exercise with thirty minutes of prayer and Bible study every day, imagine the kind of fitness you could achieve! Think about that. I challenge you to do that and to glorify God in your body while truly enjoying life to the fullest.

*   *   *   *   *

That's *my* challenge to you as well. We're not to obsess over our physical fitness because it is not an end in itself but simply a means to the end of glorifying God and enjoying to the fullest the life He has given us. Paul told Timothy, "Train yourself for godliness; for while bodily training is of some value, godliness is of value in every way, as it holds promise for the present life and also for the life to come" (1 Timothy 4:7–8). Physical and spiritual training is not an either/or proposition but both/and.

With Ken Cooper's challenge before us, let me share two more brief points as we wrap up our thoughts on physical fitness.

THANK GOD FOR YOUR HEALTH AND REFUSE TO DWELL ON PROBLEMS

The human mind is so powerful that we can convince ourselves we are sick when there is no physical reason for illness. I reject the teaching that God's will for each of us is always health and prosperity and that therefore any sickness is outside of His will. But I do believe that if we constantly entertain sick thoughts about ourselves, we are going to be sick.

We all know people who love to talk about their physical problems to anyone who will listen. You know better than to ask them how they're feeling because you're going to get an organ recital about their heart, kidneys, liver, and so on. Hypochondria is an old problem, and it's all in the mind—although I did hear about one hypochondriac whose tombstone announced, "I told you I was sick."

When I was in seminary, about four or five of my buddies and I decided to conduct an experiment on another friend. We decided we were all going to tell him at different times of the day how bad he looked, and before the day was over, he went home sick. Thoughts of sickness can produce sick bodies. Don't tell yourself you are sick. Tell yourself you are well.

Of course, sometimes sickness comes, and there are many faithful and dynamic servants of God whose bodies are not healthy. But so many times great believers who have real physical problems they could talk about are the least likely to dwell on them and the first to talk about the grace and power of God to sustain them and the wonderful things He is doing. Come to think of it, the apostle Paul stands out as an example of this kind of person. I want to be like him.

TRUST IN THE HEALING, LIFE-GIVING POWER OF JESUS CHRIST

When I use the term *healing*, I'm not just thinking of Christ's power to heal illness and restore someone to health, although I believe with all my heart in His power to do that. God's healing and restoring power also refers to the way He renews our bodies and strength each day. This is the promise of Scripture: "They who wait for the LORD shall renew their strength; they shall mount up with wings like eagles; they shall run and not be weary; they shall walk and not faint" (Isaiah 40:31).

We are actually being healed every day as our bodies that God has "fearfully and wonderfully made" (Psalm 139:14) fight off cancer cells and other diseases. In the final analysis, being physically fit is another way to praise and honor God for some of His most amazing gifts, our bodies. The Bible exhorts us, "Whatever you do, work heartily, as for the Lord and not for men" (Colossians 3:23).

That "whatever" can include exercising and practicing discipline in our eating and drinking in order to maximize the life God has given us. As a well-known commercial for cholesterol medicine (Zocor) says, "It's your future. Be there!"

PART TWO

Getting Started

CHAPTER FIVE

Your Life's Message

It's amazing how quickly certain words, phrases, and acronyms become part of our everyday language and culture. Consider the letters HDTV—high-definition television, also referred to simply as HD. This technology is already so familiar that many times a television program will have a small icon in the corner of the picture telling viewers that this particular program is available in HD. That's all that needs to be said because these letters mean that this program can be seen in the clearest, sharpest picture possible.

If you've watched a program or sports event in high definition as opposed to conventional television, you know what an amazing difference it makes. I don't know exactly how HDTV works, but I know that watching an event on it is like being there and is in some ways even better than being there.

Philippians 1:27 describes high-definition Christian living—a life that is bolder, richer, and clearer for Christ. Paul writes:

> *Only let your manner of life be worthy of the gospel of Christ, so that whether I come and see you or am absent, I may hear of you that you are standing firm in one spirit, with one mind striving side by side for the faith of the gospel.*

YOUR LIFE'S MESSAGE NEEDS TO BE CENTERED IN THE GOSPEL

This text tells us what the Christian's basic life message ought to be. By putting the word translated "only" at the beginning of verse 27, Paul was saying in effect, "There's just one thing that's really important. Don't miss what I'm going to say." Then he stated the importance of our being a living witness for the gospel, the good news of the death, burial, and resurrection of Jesus Christ for our sins.

The verb translated "let your manner of life," or "live your life," is interesting because it contains the root form *poli*, which you may recognize. This is the basis of our word *politics* and is also used in the New Testament for the concept of citizenship. All of these words refer to government, which is responsible for the proper conduct and administration of life. The Greek word *polis* means "city," as in Minneapolis or Indianapolis.

The Philippians were familiar with this word because they were a colony of Rome, and as such they were citizens of the Roman Empire. Paul used a kind of play on words here by saying, "As citizens of Philippi and Rome, you are also citizens of God's heavenly empire, His Kingdom. Live your lives, perform your duty, in a manner that is worthy of the gospel." Our first allegiance as believers is to God and His Kingdom.

We Need to Define the Gospel to Those Who Embrace It

Paul gave a sweeping view of the priority that the gospel is to have in our lives by using several key words and concepts earlier in the first chapter of Philippians. One is the *fellowship* of the gospel. This is a word that's familiar to many—*koinonia*, "fellowship," which is at the very heart of the Christian faith. Philippians 1:5 refers to their "partnership [*koinonia*] in the gospel" that Paul valued so much. As Christians we share a common life, a common faith in Christ. Knowing Him and making Him known through the gospel is what brings us together, and so our fellowship is truly in the gospel. The good news of Jesus Christ is what we ought to be excited about and talking about when we come together.

Then in Philippians 1:12 Paul spoke of the *furtherance* of the gospel, which was his own life's purpose: "what has happened to me has really served to advance the gospel." Advancing the gospel to the ends of the earth is the purpose of every Christian. Paul could be content and even joyful in his pain and imprisonment because he knew his circumstances were advancing the gospel.

There is also the *force* of the gospel, which we read about in Philippians 1:16: "I am put here for the defense of the gospel." He may have been referring to his entire life's work or more specifically his imprisonment, through which he had a chance to share the gospel with authorities in the Roman Empire. But either way, the important thing to him was the defense of the gospel. We'll have more to say about this below.

Then we read about the *faith* of the gospel at the end of Philippians 1:27. This has to do with the essential content of our faith, which is the gospel. The core of the gospel is stated very clearly in Scripture: "I delivered to you as of first importance what I also received: that Christ died for our sins in accordance with the Scriptures, that he was buried, that he was raised on the third day in accordance with the Scriptures" (1 Corinthians 15:3–4).

That is the gospel clearly stated in high definition. Christ took our sins upon Himself on the cross as He died in our place, bearing our judgment and our hell. Then having been buried to prove He was dead and not simply unconscious, on the third day He rose again. Without the death, burial, and resurrection of Jesus Christ, there is no Christian faith.

Before we can make the gospel our life's message and communicate it clearly and passionately to others by our words and lifestyle, we have to understand the place it should occupy in our lives. As Paul said to the Corinthians, the gospel is "of first importance."

We Need to Defend the Gospel Against Those Who Attack It

Despite what a lot of people would like to believe, the gospel is not whatever we want it to be. It is not an empty basket into which we can dump whatever ideas or terms we want to use. Since the gospel has specific content, anything else that goes under the name of Christianity is not the faith of Christ. Therefore, delivering our life's message accurately and fully involves defending the gospel.

There are two basic attacks against the gospel in our world today. The first assault is made by those who distort the message of salvation. One very common form of distortion is adding some kind of works system to the finished work of Christ so that the truth of salvation by grace alone and faith alone is obscured.

Entire religious systems are built on the distorted doctrine of doing good works to earn heaven. I'm not talking about other world religions, but about groups we call cults that claim the name of Christ and purport to have other revelations from God that supposedly correct or supersede the Bible.

This is nothing new because in his day Paul also battled those who wanted to add something else to the gospel. They were the Judaizers, who wanted to make Gentile believers add the requirements of the Mosaic Law, particularly circumcision, to the gospel of grace. Paul wasn't very charitable to these people, calling them "dogs" and "evil-doers" (Philippians 3:2). When the purity of the gospel and people's eternal destiny are at stake, doctrinal error and those who teach it cannot be tolerated.

A second major attack on the gospel is made by those who dilute the message of Christ by watering it down. These are the people who never mention sin and the need for repentance in their gospel. There's no hell, only heaven; just say a prayer or believe in God. People who preach a diluted gospel may even talk about accepting Jesus, but without the admission of sin and genuine repentance there is no gospel and no salvation.

My purpose is not to criticize people's motives but to evaluate their message. We can't be fuzzy or indecisive here because the gospel is clear, and there is so much at stake. The gospel is not an intellectual belief in Jesus or an emotional response to His claims. The gospel is coming to the place in your life where you recognize your desperate need of salvation and your utter lostness as a sinner, you turn from your sin in repentance, and you trust Christ's sacrifice on the cross and nothing else for your salvation. This is the gospel that Paul said is "the power of God for salvation to everyone who believes" (Romans 1:16).

I continue to celebrate the power of the gospel to change lives. One person who has experienced this radical transformation is Pat Summerall, the well-known television sportscaster who was a fixture with John Madden on pro football broadcasts for many years. Talk about someone with a life message to communicate! Pat has an inspiring testimony of God's grace in his life.

Pat battled alcoholism for most of his life. Several years ago he was looking in the mirror when he realized that his life was falling apart and he knew he had to do something. So he cried out to God in desperation, and the amazing grace of the Lord Jesus Christ met Pat right where he was. He was delivered from his sin and from alcoholism and became a new creation in Christ.

But then in 2004 Pat faced a severe health crisis and needed a liver transplant. He nearly died, and by all accounts probably should have died, but he received a new liver and within one year was playing golf again and was back on the air. Later Pat and I were sharing dinner with our wives one evening when he said, "Jack, I want to share something with you. I didn't know why God preserved my life when I needed a liver. I wondered why I was still here when so many people die of liver disease without receiving a transplant. I realized that someone else had to die so I could live, and I really struggled with that. I kept asking God, 'Why am I here? Why am I still alive?'"

At that point Pat reached into his pocket and pulled out a well-worn piece of paper. "This is the second page of your book." I looked at it and realized the paper was from the page proofs of my book *Becoming a Man of God: Essential Priorities of a Man's Life*, which would be released a little later that year. I had asked Pat to endorse the book, and he had underlined a paragraph on page 2. He told me, "I was reading the book on an airplane, and when I read this particular paragraph I realized why I'm here, what my purpose is."

Now I would like to tell you that this paragraph was a very profound and powerful thought. But it was a very simple statement that our purpose in life is to give our best for Jesus Christ and to use our lives to the glory of God. Pat told me how these words resonated in his soul and gave him the purpose he had been seeking. He also said that whenever he speaks, he closes with the words from that paragraph.

I praise God that Pat Summerall found God's amazing grace. All of us who know Christ have received a transplant because Someone died to provide us with His eternal life in place of our spiritual death. The gospel must be defended against being distorted or diluted because it alone is the power of God for the salvation of everyone who believes.

YOUR CHARACTER NEEDS TO REFLECT WELL ON THE GOSPEL

Over the past few years, we have seen more than enough examples of people whose lives did not match their "life's message" in terms of what they claimed to believe or stand for. You may remember a rash of instances several years ago in which some very high-profile people, including the newly hired football coach at Notre Dame University, were discredited and lost their jobs when it was discovered that they had lied on their résumés. We even watched as a former President of the United States lied publicly about a private sexual affair that turned out to be all too true.

Such duplicity has no place in the Christian life. The key in Philippians 1:27 is to live a life that is "worthy" of the gospel. Elsewhere Paul exhorted believers to live with integrity so that we "may adorn the doctrine of God our Savior" (Titus 2:10). The idea is to make the gospel attractive to unbelievers as they see the positive difference it has made in our lives.

Every Christian is delivering a message to the world about what we believe and how it affects the way we live. There's an old saying with a lot of truth to it that goes something like this: "What you *are* is speaking to me so loudly I can't hear what you're saying." The shorthand version of this is probably more familiar: "Actions speak louder than words."

Of course, for us as Christians it's not an either/or proposition when it comes to delivering our life's message. We need to proclaim the gospel with our lips as well as with our lives. Paul's instruction is to make sure the two match up, which is where the issue of integrity and character of life comes in.

It's Important to Make Sure That Each Part of Your Life Rings True

My longtime friend O. S. Hawkins has a helpful grid we can use to see how integrity works. He divides life into four areas where we need to display integrity of life and witness.

The first of these is our *public life*. This is where most people know us, including casual friends, neighbors, acquaintances, and people we meet. Our public life is the persona or image that we portray to others.

We also have a *professional life*. This is where we relate to others primarily in our careers or businesses, whatever our particular calling may be.

A third area is our *personal life* that we live before a small group of family and intimate friends who really know us well. Your spouse and children know the most about you because they see you in a realm to which the public and your business contacts don't usually have access.

The fourth area is our *private life*. This is the world of our inner self, the part of us that only God really sees and knows. This is where the issue of integrity gets tough because while we can fool others and even ourselves, God knows whether our words and deeds are true.

Your Integrity Will Give Your Life's Message Real Validity

A person who is living with integrity in these four areas has a message that's worth hearing. Integrity means that I am the same person no matter who I am with or where I am. It means that I tell the truth and take responsibility for my life and my actions. It means that I am willing to do the right thing even when it is not easy and when others around me are taking the easy way out. Integrity means that I possess honor and decency, that I'm faithful in the small things as well as in the big things.

That's why it is so critical that our private or inner life be worthy of the gospel. It's the small things that often trip us up because we have not developed and deepened our character to withstand temptation. Our enemy Satan is on the prowl, looking for someone to devour (1 Peter 5:8). And while we're not to be afraid of him, neither can we afford to ignore his roar. In the final analysis, integrity is an inside job.

LET'S TAKE OFF THE MASKS AND LIVE AUTHENTICALLY FOR JESUS CHRIST

In the ancient world actors had to play several roles; so they would wear masks as they assumed different characters. This play-acting behind a mask came to be used in the New Testament to describe people who pretended to be something they really weren't on the inside. This was called hypocrisy, and it's still with us today. I've been a pastor a long time, and through the years I've seen people wear masks and play roles in an attempt to appear pious and spiritual. But men or women of character don't need to play a part. They simply are what they are, and their life's message rings true.

Is It in You?

I love those Gatorade commercials that show athletes drinking that sports drink and turning the color of the drink as they perspire. And then the question is asked, "Is it in you?" That's a question we ought to ask ourselves in terms of the way our lives are displaying the character of Christ. We need to examine ourselves because when we are stressed and sweating and under pressure, what's on the inside will come out. That's why we need to drink deeply of the life that Christ gives through the Holy Spirit who lives within us.

Is the character of Christ in you? That's what people really want to know about our faith. They want to see the real thing come out of us when the pressure is on. Since all of us are delivering some kind of life message every day, our responsibility is to make sure we are living lives that are worthy of the gospel.

Your credibility with others is crucial. Whether you're a leader in the church, in business, or in your home, you have a distinct sphere of influence. The people who are watching and following you need to see a life's message from you that is genuine.

Your Life's Message Can Have Tremendous Influence on Others

There was a young Jewish boy many years ago in Germany whose family was very religious and went to synagogue every week. But when the boy was a young teenager they moved to another German town that did not have a synagogue. There was only a Lutheran church there, which was attended by the influential people of that town. This boy and his family were shocked and stunned when the father came in one day and announced that they were joining the Lutheran church. When asked why, he said, "Because it's good for business."

This young teenage boy was very disappointed that his father's religion meant so little to him. The boy became angry, hostile, and cynical.

He ended up in England studying at the university and could be seen every day at the British Museum, writing and reading. This young man ultimately produced a book and a worldview that changed the history of the world. His worldview had no place for God or religion. In fact, he declared religion to be "the opiate of the masses."

This Jewish man's ideas began to be read and adopted by other thinkers and revolutionaries, and they were the driving force behind the Russian revolution of 1917. His views were known as Socialism or Communism, and now the world knows his name—Karl Marx. World history was changed, and millions were enslaved for decades because of a father whose life did not yield a consistent, believable message.

Karl Marx is a radical example of the importance of living consistently with our faith. But let's also remind ourselves of the tremendously positive and godly impact we can make when we live with integrity. The best argument for the gospel is a follower of Christ who is full of joy, full of faith, and lives the faith. A godly man or woman living in a way that is worthy of the gospel of Jesus is a powerful weapon in the hand of God.

The imagery of an athlete straining in competition is actually the picture Paul had in mind in Philippians 1:27 when he said we should be "striving side by side for the faith of the gospel." The Greek word translated "striving" is an athletic word. It illustrates a runner straining to break the tape at the finish line and win the race. Paul's words resonated in Philippi because the people saw how consistently he lived and labored for Christ and the gospel. As we follow Christ, let us run hard to Him and for Him so that others may see and hear the good news. They want to see Christians who are consistent and credible in their faith, so let's give them a clear, sharp, high-definition picture of the difference the gospel can make in our, and their, lives!

CHAPTER SIX

The Mighty Cross

Some baseball fans might have been confused if they had tuned in to the middle of a Los Angeles Dodgers game early in April 2007. Every member of the Dodgers was wearing number 42 on the back of his uniform that day, and for good reason.

This was part of Major League Baseball's official celebration of the life and legacy of Jackie Robinson, the man who broke baseball's color line by becoming the first African-American player in the Majors. Robinson joined the then Brooklyn Dodgers in 1947; so the celebration was marking the sixtieth anniversary of his courageous accomplishment.

It was fitting that each of the Dodgers wore Robinson's old uniform number, as did several players on the opposing team. In fact, any Major League player who wanted to was allowed to wear number 42 on that day—which was significant because 42 was officially retired in all of Major League Baseball several years ago in honor of Jackie Robinson.

What those Dodgers and other players did was a wonderful demonstration of solidarity and team spirit in honor of someone special. The members of a team are supposed to be one in mind and spirit, and on Jackie Robinson Day those players wore a visible symbol of their unity.

It was also interesting to hear several other African-American baseball greats credit Robinson as being their example for the way he refused to be defeated by or lash out against the racism—the vicious name-calling, taunts, and threats—he faced every day. These players who came after Robinson faced their own battles against prejudice in their careers, but they told how they were determined to make it because they had seen Jackie Robinson make it and they knew it could be done.

This remarkable story holds valuable illustrations for us in our daily Christian lives. As I read Philippians 2:1–8 I see several parallels. One of the lessons is the demonstration of teamwork and like-mindedness that Paul prayed for in the church of Jesus Christ. He told the believers at Philippi:

> *Complete my joy by being of the same mind, having the same love, being in full accord and of one mind. Do nothing from rivalry or conceit, but in humility count others more significant than yourselves. Let each of you look not only to his own interests, but also to the interests of others. (Philippians 2:2–4)*

Paul expressed this desire for humble, loving unity among God's people because the church's unity is both the key to our witness and effectiveness and the will of God. In His high-priestly prayer the night before His crucifixion, Jesus prayed four times that believers would be "one" (John 17:11, 21–23).

Jesus set the standard of humility and a servant attitude that is necessary for true unity to exist in His body.

But Paul's appeal to the church for unity also set the context for one of the most magnificent passages in all of Scripture:

> *Have this mind among yourselves, which is yours in Christ Jesus, who, though he was in the form of God, did not count equality with God a thing to be grasped, but made himself nothing, taking the form of a servant, being born in the likeness of men. And being found in human form, he humbled himself by becoming obedient to the point of death, even death on a cross. (Philippians 2:5–8, emphasis added)*

I wanted you to see this text in its entirety because it was likely a divinely inspired hymn of confession and faith that was sung in the first-century church. It actually extends through verse 11, but we're going to save verses 9–11 for the next chapter because they deal with Christ's exaltation. The emphasis of verses 5–8 is His condescension and humiliation in veiling His deity to come to earth as a humble Servant and die an agonizing death on the cross for our sins. This great hymn, often called the *kenosis* for reasons I'll explain later, is full of great theology about Jesus Christ and also holds a great responsibility and ethical charge to all of us who truly want to be fit for life.

JESUS IS GOD, COEQUAL AND COETERNAL WITH THE FATHER

Let's consider Christ's deity, which is where Paul begins in this amazing passage of Scripture. Several times during Jesus' ministry on earth, people asked the question, "Who then is this?" (for example, Mark 4:41). The disciples were overwhelmed when Jesus stilled the storm and wondered aloud about Him because they were slow to come to grips with the fact that Jesus is Immanuel, "God with us" (Matthew 1:23).

When Jesus rode into the city of Jerusalem for His triumphal entry on Palm Sunday, the crowd greeted Him with, "Blessed is the King who comes in the name of the Lord!" (Luke 19:38), referring to His kingly status as the Son of David. Many in that crowd hoped Jesus would be Israel's political savior and deliverer to free the nation from Rome's tyranny. Others believed that Jesus was a prophet, and still others hailed Him as the Messiah.

Jesus was and is all of these things, and more. He is the eternal, uncreated God, of the same essence as and coequal with the Father and the Spirit. Jesus "was in the form of God" before He ever came to earth (Philippians 2:6). Jesus existed before time began. Jesus is not a man becoming God, for that would be impossible. Jesus is God becoming a man—fully God and fully man, the God-man.

JESUS DESCENDED FROM HIS EXALTED THRONE IN HEAVEN TO TAKE THE HUMBLEST PLACE ON EARTH

The truth of Jesus' deity makes the rest of Philippians 2 even more amazing. Paul said that Jesus "did not count equality with God a thing to be grasped, but made himself nothing" (vv. 6b–7a). The word translated "made himself nothing" introduces a profound mystery, the *kenosis* or self-emptying of Jesus Christ as it is often referred to in theological terms. The word *kenosis* means "emptying," but it does not mean that

Jesus emptied Himself of His deity when He came to earth, for that would also be impossible. This was not the subtraction of Christ's deity but rather the addition of His humanity.

Jesus Veiled His Deity in His Humanity

When Jesus took on human flesh, He willingly veiled His deity, declined to use some of His divine prerogatives in order to carry out His mission of redemption. For example, if Jesus had not veiled His glory, He would have created fear and awe in everyone He met as they came face-to-face with the God of heaven. The disciples got a brief glimpse of Jesus' glory in the Transfiguration (Matthew 17:1–8), and they were terrified and overcome.

The *kenosis* of Christ also explains how He could be subject to hunger, thirst, weariness, and all the other weaknesses and needs of a human being. Jesus did not work a miracle whenever He needed food or water, nor did He move supernaturally from place to place but walked the long miles. And He did not snap His fingers and instantly incinerate all of His enemies. Even His appearance was that of an ordinary man, as the prophet foretold: "He had no form or majesty that we should look at him, and no beauty that we should desire him" (Isaiah 53:2). The Son of God was viewed as a common man.

Jesus Suffered Great Humiliation to Become One of Us

The act by which the Second Person of the Trinity became a man is often called the humiliation of Christ. No other term does justice to the concept of God taking on weak, human flesh. Even if Jesus had come to earth as the greatest and most exalted King and Leader ever, adored by the world, His incarnation would still have been a humiliating step down from His highly exalted position as the sovereign God. A wonderful old hymn called "Down from His Glory" portrays Christ's condescension:

> *Down from His glory, ever living story,*
> *My God and Savior came, and Jesus was His name;*
> *Born in a manger, to His own a stranger,*
> *A Man of sorrows, tears and agony!*

O how I love Him! How I adore Him!
My breath, my sunshine, my all in all.
The great Creator became my Savior,
And all of God's fullness dwelleth in Him!

What condescension, bringing us redemption,
That in the dead of night, not one faint hope in sight,
God, gracious, tender, laid aside His splendor,
Stooping to win, to woo, to save my soul!
(Chorus)

Without reluctance, flesh and blood His substance,
He took the form of man, revealed His hidden plan;
O glorious mystery, sacrifice of Calvary,
And now I know Thou art the great "I AM."
(Chorus)

Praise God for the awesome mystery of Christ's descent to earth to be our Savior! Paul continued in Philippians 2:7–8 by using several terms that give us further insight into Jesus' condescension. Jesus took on human "likeness" and "form," two words that indicate He was fully human and did not merely appear to be in the flesh, as one early heresy in the church taught. In fact, the word "form" used in verse 8 to describe Jesus' humanity is the same word used in verse 6 where we are told Jesus was in the form of God. Therefore, to deny Jesus' full humanity is to deny His full deity because they are inseparably linked.

But Jesus' humiliation did not end at His becoming a man. He also became a "servant" who "humbled himself . . . to the point of death." And not just any death, but "death on a cross" (Philippians 2:8)—the most humiliating and excruciating way a person in that day could die.

Jesus Came to Die a Sacrificial Death for Our Sins

Why did Jesus willingly accept all the limitations of humanity and the loss of His high position? Why was He willing to go to the cross? As one song says, "He did it all for me." John the Baptist proclaimed of Jesus, "Behold, the Lamb of God, who takes away the sin of the world!" (John 1:29). We're going to spend the last half of this chapter considering

Christ's sacrificial death. But can you imagine the depths of God's love and the lengths to which He would go to express that love?

A few years ago my wife, Deb, bought some goldfish she had been wanting. A couple of them died, and one was left, a little fish named Noah that Deb really cared about. She fed that one last fish every day and cleaned out his bowl, and Noah thrived.

One day Deb was cleaning out Noah's bowl when she accidentally dropped him down the garbage disposal in the kitchen. She let out a scream, and I came running in to see what had happened. When I found out where Noah was, I thought, *Well, Noah has seen his last flood.* But Deb wasn't ready to let her little lost fish go. She took her soft, lovely hand and thrust it down into that garbage disposal to rescue Noah.

Now I didn't know what kind of muck was in the bottom of that disposal, and I didn't want to find out. But Deb never hesitated—and sure enough, she pulled out little Noah alive, cleaned him off, and put him back in his bowl, where he swam happily and went on to live a happy life.

Why on earth would someone as lovely as my wife stick her hand down into the mess of a garbage disposal to save a fish? Only one reason—that little fish was so valuable to her that he was worth rescuing even when he had slid into the mire and was heading for sure death. I tell you that story to remind you of something much greater: God Almighty thrust not just His hand but His beloved, sinless Son down into the garbage of this world, reaching down into the depths of our humanity and depravity, suffering an agonizing and humiliating death on the cross, all to rescue us because we are of infinite worth to Him. "O glorious mystery, sacrifice of Calvary!"

JESUS DIED AN EXCRUCIATING DEATH ON THE CROSS TO SECURE OUR SALVATION

We have seen Jesus' deity and descent profiled in Philippians 2:5–8. The third part of the story of Calvary is Jesus' death on the cross. Paul said that Jesus went to the cross in obedience to the Father, another statement in this marvelous passage that is truly incomprehensible. Jesus Himself said, "I lay down my life that I may take it up again. No one takes it from me, but I lay it down of my own accord" (John

10:17b–18a). Notice that Jesus was also willing to die for us. His obedience to the Father was given gladly, not grudgingly.

There is a world of meaning and suffering in the phrase, "even death on a cross" (Philippians 2:8). Jesus did not die an easy death or slip away peacefully in His sleep after a long life. He was brutally tortured and tormented, then nailed on a crude cross raised up and dropped into a hole in the earth in an area on the outskirts of Jerusalem that was essentially a garbage heap.

It's amazing to realize the transformation that the cross has undergone over the centuries as the primary symbol of Christianity. It has become an art object, rendered in beautiful paintings or cast in gold and encrusted with jewels in some cases. Even the wooden crosses in many of our churches are beautifully crafted. And, of course, the cross has become a very popular piece of jewelry even for people who have no particular allegiance to Jesus Christ. Many of us *wear* the cross, but we are often much less willing to *bear* the cross.

Humanly speaking, the cross was repulsive. The beauty of the cross is not in the instrument itself, for it was a cruel killing device. The Bible says that Jesus "endured the cross, despising the shame" (Hebrews 12:2). The beauty of the cross was in the One who hung on it, He who is altogether lovely. Consider these features of Jesus' death on the cross.

Jesus' Death Was a Violent Death

Jesus' death was first and foremost a very violent one. Producer Mel Gibson has given our generation an unforgettable picture of this in his movie *The Passion of the Christ*. It received an "R" rating for violence, and most moviegoers could not look upon the portrayal of Jesus' suffering without breaking down. And yet I believe the brutality of that movie did not do full justice to the violence that was unleashed upon the sinless Son of God. I earlier referred to Jesus' death as excruciating, a word that comes from the Greek word for *crucifixion*.

Jesus' Death Was a Voluntary Death

This is the glorious truth that Jesus spoke of in John 10:18 concerning His death. Paul called it an "obedient" death in Philippians 2:8. Jesus' death was neither an accident nor an afterthought in the mind of God.

Jesus stepped forward in the council halls of heaven in eternity past and said, "I will go and give My life for the salvation of lost sinners." The Bible says that Jesus, the Lamb of God, was slain "before the foundation of the world" (Revelation 13:8).

But why the cross? Because, and I say this respectfully, God was facing a dilemma. How could He who is holy redeem and have a relationship with people who are sinful? How could He be both "just" and at the same time "the justifier of the one who has faith in Jesus" (Romans 3:26)? The answer was for God to transfer the sins of the world onto His own Son and send Him to earth to die for our salvation.

The Triune Godhead sitting in divine session drew up the plan of salvation, and the Son became the volunteer sacrifice to provide salvation to all who believe. He chose obedience even to the death of the cross.

Jesus' Death Was a Vicarious Death

Jesus died a vicarious death because He took your place and mine on the cross. Paul explained it this way: "For our sake he [God] made him [Jesus] to be sin who knew no sin, so that in him we might become the righteousness of God" (2 Corinthians 5:21).

The Bible's teaching on the vicarious, substitutionary death of Christ is a precious truth that has come under constant attack from people both inside and outside the church. I can readily understand the critics in the world. It is very offensive to human pride to be told that the bloody, violent death of Jesus was the death we deserved because of our wickedness, rebellion, and sin. It's much nicer just to say that Jesus died as our example to show us the beauty of sacrifice and show us how to die. That way people don't have to face up to the fact that Jesus died as their substitute, taking the death and hell they deserved.

Of course, the church has also never lacked for critics within its walls who deny the teaching of Scripture. Liberal theologians have long objected to the vicarious nature of Christ's death, usually preferring the example theory of the atonement as I described it above. That way they can hold on to their own pride and also avoid having to tell the people in their churches the nasty truth that they are lost sinners without hope apart from the blood of Christ.

But Jesus paid our sin-debt on the cross—a debt so horrific that only an eternity in hell can satisfy it. Don't let anyone talk you out of the truth of Christ's substitutionary death. Any athlete knows what substitution means. When the coach sends a player in to substitute for you, that player isn't just your example. He's your *replacement*, there to do the job for you and, hopefully, help win the victory for the team. Thank God that our replacement is Jesus, the only One who can do the job and win the victory for us.

Jesus' Death Was a Victorious Death

The cross was not a defeat for Jesus, but the means to a glorious victory that culminated in His resurrection. Jesus triumphed in and over the cross. Paul declared, "He disarmed the rulers and authorities and put them to open shame" by the cross (Colossians 2:15). Elsewhere the apostle said that the powers of this world did not understand the wisdom of God by which He defeated His foes, "for if they had, they would not have crucified the Lord of glory" (1 Corinthians 2:8).

Oh, the wonderful cross! Jesus turned it from a symbol of torture and death into a symbol of life. Jesus conquered sin, death, and hell when He cried out on the cross, "*Tetelestai,*" which means, "It is finished" (John 19:30).

No team plans for defeat. Defeat is what happens when your plan for victory fails. Jesus' cry from the cross was not the cry of a defeated victim, but the shout of a conquering King who took power over the domain of Satan and all the enemies of the cross. And the wonderful thing is that we share in Christ's victory over sin today, and someday we will share in His victory over death.

WE ARE TO CARRY OUR OWN CROSS IN RESPONSE TO JESUS' EXAMPLE

There's another thing we need to remember about the cross. There is a cross for you and me to carry. Jesus said, "If anyone would come after me, let him deny himself and take up his cross daily and follow me" (Luke 9:23).

Remember that the context of Philippians 2:5–8 is an appeal for us to have the same attitude as Jesus. What was that attitude? One of humility, surrender, and sacrifice, even to death on the cross. We have a picture of carrying the cross in the story of Simon of Cyrene, who was pulled out of the crowd and forced to carry Jesus' cross (Matthew 27:32).

For one brief moment Simon was given the greatest privilege a human being could ever know—to carry the cross of Jesus Christ. That is our daily calling and compelling privilege today. We need to say like Paul, "Far be it from me to boast except in the cross of our Lord Jesus Christ, by which the world has been crucified to me, and I to the world" (Galatians 6:14).

What does it mean to carry our cross? The same thing it meant for Jesus: death. Being dead to the world, and the world being dead to us, means that we must be willing to die each day to ourselves—our selfish ambitions, our sinful desires, and whatever else keeps us from following Christ with our whole hearts and lives.

So many people are trying to find themselves. I know this is countercultural, but the cross calls us to deny ourselves. The world says, "Promote yourself, push yourself out in front, please yourself." But Jesus says, "Give yourself, deny yourself, lose your life so that you may find life in Me."

The way up for the Christian is down. The Bible says, "Humble yourselves, therefore, under the mighty hand of God so that at the proper time he may exalt you" (1 Peter 5:6). We descend into the greatness of Christ when we give ourselves to follow Him, and we are thus lifted up and exalted with Him. And one day we will be with Him forever because we dared to follow the Christ of the cross.

There are only two ways to live. Either we say to Jesus, "Not my will, but Yours be done," or He says to us, "Not My will, but yours be done." I urge you to have the same attitude as Christ, who took up His cross and carried it all the way to Calvary for you.

CHAPTER SEVEN

Jesus the Lord of Life

Golf fans will remember that the 2004 Masters tournament was held during Holy Week, with the final round being played on April 11, which was Easter Sunday.

Real golf fans may know that this wasn't the first time Easter and one of golf's most prestigious events fell on the same day. One year when this occurred, the producer of the television coverage for the tournament was said to be irate when he discovered the conflict, wondering how such a major religious holiday could be scheduled for the same day as the climactic final round of the Masters. The story goes that he called his staff together and told them to go find out who scheduled Easter and ask them to change the date so it wouldn't conflict with the television broadcast.

I don't know what that television producer's staff came up with, but I know they weren't able to move Easter because they weren't the ones who called for a celebration of the resurrection. The One who brought about Easter is Jesus, the risen Lord of life! Jesus is the only person who has gone to the grave and come back to tell us about life and death, and He is the only person who can say, "All authority in heaven and on earth has been given to me" (Matthew 28:18).

It's amazing how excited we get about events that seem so important in our world. But above and beyond every event and person in either time or eternity stands Jesus Christ—who died and was buried, but who rose again and sits exalted at the right hand of the Father in heaven.

The world cannot ignore Jesus, and in fact His life has been the subject of countless news features the past few years, along with several best-selling books and a major Hollywood motion picture. Granted, much of this media and literary attention has been focused on trying to discredit the Gospel accounts of Jesus' life and death—without any success, I might add. *The Da Vinci Code*, *The Gospel of Judas*, and *The Hidden Gospels* are just three examples of the popular attention being devoted to Jesus Christ. Just as all the hype over these books was dying down, the announcement came out of Israel that "Jesus' bones have been found." Of course, that whole claim was a hoax and publicity stunt.

I didn't lose any sleep over what those books or that burial box in Israel might reveal, and I hope you didn't either. But these things are a reminder that everywhere we go, people are talking about Jesus. It seems that everybody has an opinion about who Jesus is and why He came. Was He a rabbi? Was He a reformer? Was He a revolutionary? It's a question that everyone must answer, a question Jesus asked concerning Himself: "What do you think about the Christ? Whose son is he?" (Matthew 22:42). And once we are settled on who Jesus is, we must make a decision about Him. Even Pilate asked at Jesus' trial, "What shall I do with Jesus who is called Christ?" (Matthew 27:22).

In Philippians 2:5–11 we find the only answer that really matters concerning Jesus. It is given in this clear testimony of Jesus' deity and humanity that was, as we said in the previous chapter, most likely a hymn to the Lord Jesus Christ sung by the early Christians.

JESUS HAS BEEN EXALTED TO THE HIGHEST PLACE IN HEAVEN, WHERE HE REIGNS AS LORD

In his great sermon on the Day of Pentecost, Peter said that even though Jesus had been put to death by evil men, "God raised him up, loosing the pangs of death, because it was not possible for him to be held by it" (Acts 2:24). Jesus as the God-man humbled Himself even to death on a cross, but it was impossible for Him not to be raised and exalted because He is the eternal God. Philippians 2:5–8 speaks of Jesus' deity, descent, and death. The last stanza of the hymn (vv. 9–11) speaks of His exaltation:

Therefore God has highly exalted him and bestowed on him the name that is above every name, so that at the name of Jesus every knee should bow, in heaven and on earth and under the earth, and every tongue confess that Jesus Christ is Lord, to the glory of God the Father.

If I only had one message to deliver to the world, it would be this: Jesus Christ is Lord! That's the message everyone needs to hear, because God the Father has given Jesus the name that is above every name and has decreed that every knee will bow to Him. And this will happen, whether people bow willingly today in surrender and commitment or are forced to bow at the judgment and confess with their mouths what they refused to confess in life—Jesus is Lord!

There have been many names of significance in history, but there is no name like the name of Jesus. His name will stand when every other name in history has dissolved into oblivion and every enemy of the cross is vanquished.

One of these names from the dustbin of history is François-Marie Arouet, better known to the world by his pen name, Voltaire. This noted eighteenth-century French intellectual and bitter atheist boasted that within a hundred years of his death, Christianity would be a relic preserved only in museums. Yet in 1805, fewer than twenty years after Voltaire died in 1788, the French Bible Society was organized and began its activities. And we are told that a hundred years after Voltaire's death, his former home was being used by the Society to store and distribute Bibles.

To put it in today's context, you can get a Bible at Wal-Mart, but I seriously doubt if you'll find Voltaire's writings there. His boast has been forgotten, but Jesus still reigns as Lord.

Jesus' Name Was Vindicated after the Humiliation of the Cross

Considering the fact that many people work their entire lives to make a name for themselves, the exaltation of Jesus' name is even more remarkable when you consider His earthly ministry. He never wrote a song, a poem, or a book, and yet the world's libraries are filled with songs, poems, and books about Him. He didn't build any buildings or establish a famous school. He didn't even build a church, and yet there are schools and churches and countless other buildings around the world dedicated to His name and built to perpetuate His work.

Jesus also spent His entire life in a tiny country, never traveling more than about two hundred miles from His home, but He is the most well-known person of history. He never spoke to more than a few thousand people at a time, and yet today His followers number over one billion. And even though His earthly ministry lasted only a few years, its impact two thousand years later is still growing. Without question, Jesus Christ is the most dominating force and personality in human history. There is only one explanation for all of this: God has given Jesus a name like no other.

Jesus' name is *exalted* because it is infinitely higher than every other name. Jesus' name is *exclusive* because He is the one and only, standing completely apart from all others. Jesus' name is also *endearing* to the countless millions who have fallen at His feet in adoration and worship. And Jesus' name is *eternal*, because He was and is the ever-living God.

Philippians 2:9 begins with "Therefore," which ties what follows with the preceding context. This verse answers the question of why God highly exalted Jesus. We've already discussed one reason—the impossibility of His being held by death and remaining in His state of humiliation. A second reason for Jesus' exaltation was His complete obedience to His Father, even to death on the cross. But there is a third reason that has to do with what happened to Jesus while He was on earth.

The court of human and religious opinion and the judgment halls of Rome had deemed Jesus to be worthy of death. He was tried and sentenced to be crucified, a death that had previously been reserved for thieves, murderers, rebels, and the like. Jesus was treated as a guilty man would be treated, but on the third day His conviction was overturned in the Supreme Court of heaven when He arose. It was impossible for God to let the world's guilty verdict against His sinless Son stay on the books.

So God highly exalted Jesus, not only clearing His name, as it were, but giving Him the name that is above every name.

The Name of Jesus Stands for All That He Is and Does

At least four truths about Jesus help us understand why His name is exalted above all. The first is because of *His Person*. Jesus is the eternal Son of God who was born of a virgin and lived a sinless life. Satan attacked Jesus with all of the weaponry of hell, yet Jesus never sinned (Matthew 4:1–11). Jesus was able to stand before His accusers and say, "Which one of you convicts me of sin?" (John 8:46).

Imagine any one of us standing in front of our families and the friends who know us best, to say nothing of our enemies, and daring anyone to prove that we have done anything wrong. Jesus was not actually the One on trial before the Jewish and Roman authorities; they were the ones on trial. No one could lay any sin at Jesus' feet. The decision they had to make, and that we have to make, is not just whether Jesus is the Son of God, but what we are going to do in response to His Person.

There was a man in Jesus' inner circle of disciples who had questions about who He was and why He had come. This man's name was Thomas, and you'll remember that after the resurrection Thomas said he would not believe until He could see Jesus and touch His scars. Jesus appeared to Thomas a week later, and when Thomas saw Him he fell at Jesus' feet and confessed, "My Lord and my God!" (John 20:28), just as Paul said everyone will do someday (Philippians 2:10–11).

A second reason that Jesus' name is exalted above all others is because of *His passion*. We studied the Lord's death in detail in the previous chapter, but consider it again in light of His exaltation. Jesus came to earth the first time as our Sin-bearer, God's final sacrifice for the sin of mankind. At the cross we see the greatest demonstration of both love and hatred the world has ever known. God showed His love to sinners and at the same time showed His hatred of sin. Jesus bore that hatred and sin in His humiliation on the cross.

But here's something exciting. The Bible says that when Jesus comes again, He will not come as a Lamb to die, but as the risen Savior coming to complete our redemption: "Having been offered once to bear the sins of many, [Jesus] will appear a second time, not to deal with sin but to save those who are eagerly waiting for him" (Hebrews 9:28).

Here's a third reason for the exaltation of Jesus name: *His power*.

Do you realize the power it took to raise Jesus from the dead? Can you fathom the power it will take to cause every knee to bow and every tongue to admit that Jesus is Lord? Jesus has such power. We're told in Revelation 1:18 that because Jesus is alive He holds the keys of death and Hades, the grave.

Keys are a symbol of authority and access. I have a key that is called a grand master key. I haven't actually tried it, but I'm told this key will open every door of our church. That means I have complete access; there is no place I can't go. I have this key because the church has given me the authority to have it.

Jesus has the grand master key of the universe! Let me tell you, if anyone could come forward who had the power to prevent or reverse death and unlock the grave, he would be hailed as the greatest miracle-worker of all time. Well, such a Person has already come, and will come again.

The world is really into power and authority, and always has been. One of the most powerful men on earth during the 1930s–1950s was a rather short, stocky individual from the Republic of Georgia in what would later become the Soviet Union. He took the name Stalin, which means "steel."

Joseph Stalin held absolute power over the people he ruled. He is estimated to be responsible for the deaths of fifty-five million people. There's an amazing photo of Stalin sitting at his desk one evening, looking relaxed as he reads documents by the lamp and smokes his pipe. It could be the portrait of a great world leader tending to the affairs of state—except in this case Stalin was studying lists of names. He would go through these long lists at night, casually marking the names of those whom he wanted put to death. It is said that he would condemn as many as six thousand people to death in a single night.

We are also told that Joseph Stalin's last act on his deathbed was to raise himself from his pillow and shake his fist toward heaven. Stalin held the power of life and death over millions, but his power died with him, and today his name is reviled as the greatest mass murderer in history. And yet Jesus still reigns as Lord.

Sometimes we get discouraged as we see the power of evil in the world. But don't ever forget that the battle between good and evil is not a struggle between two equals. It's easy to miss that little phrase "under the earth" in Philippians 2:10. But that is actually a three-word declaration of Jesus' absolute power over Satan and his demons. They will bow and confess Jesus as Lord, as will every person in hell who has ever shaken a fist in the face of God. Not a single person who has ever rejected Jesus Christ will depart from God's presence without first bowing down and confessing that Jesus is Lord.

A fourth and final reason for the exaltation of Jesus' name is *His promise*. Jesus told the disciples in the Upper Room that He was leaving to prepare a place for them. Then He gave them this promise: "And if I go and prepare a place for you, I will come again and will take you to myself, that where I am you may be also" (John 14:3).

Jesus' promise was repeated by the two angels who appeared on the day He ascended into heaven in the presence of the apostles. As Jesus' feet lifted from the Mount of Olives and He disappeared into heaven, "Two men stood by them in white robes, and said, 'Men of Galilee, why do you stand looking into heaven? This Jesus, who was taken up from you into heaven, will come in the same way as you saw him go into heaven'" (Acts 1:10–11).

People ask, "What's this world coming to?" We can tell them that this world is coming to Jesus because Jesus is coming again to rule and reign and to receive the confession of everyone in heaven, on earth, and under the earth that He is Lord, to the glory of God.

EVERYTHING WE WILL EVER NEED IS AVAILABLE TO US IN JESUS' NAME

The name of Jesus is not only the name exalted above all others, but it is in His powerful name that we enjoy every blessing and benefit as His followers.

Like keys, names too are symbols of authority. In old-time movies when the soldiers ride into a village with a proclamation, the soldier in charge unfurls his document and says in a loud voice, "In the name of the exalted . . ." Then he would read the name of the king or Caesar or whatever ruler had issued the decree. That decree carried all the authority of the name that stood behind it.

One day the angels of God will unfurl His decree that the time has come for every knee to bow and every tongue to confess the exalted name of Jesus. But we do not have to wait for that day to enjoy the benefits of confessing Him as Savior.

For example, in the name of Jesus we have *authority*. Peter said to the crippled man begging at the temple gate, "In the name of Jesus Christ of Nazareth, rise up and walk!" (Acts 3:6), and the man was instantly healed.

It is also in Jesus' name that we have *atonement*, the forgiveness and cleansing of sin. One day Jesus forgave the sins of a paralyzed man lowered to Him through a roof, and those there questioned, "Why does this man speak like that? He is blaspheming! Who can forgive sins but God alone?" (Mark 2:7). They were right, of course—only God can forgive sin. And Philippians 2 declares that Jesus is God.

Jesus' name also gives us *access* to God. "We have an advocate with the Father, Jesus Christ the righteous" (1 John 2:1). We end our prayers with "in Jesus' name" not because that's what Christians are supposed to do, but as a confession that Jesus is Lord and has opened the way into heaven for us.

And it just keeps getting better. Jesus' name is also the source of our *assurance* of eternal life. Quoting the apostle John again, "I write these things to you who believe in the name of the Son of God *that you may know that you have eternal life*" (1 John 5:13, emphasis added).

Last but not least, in Jesus' name we have *assistance* for life. I love the story of Peter on the Sea of Galilee, when Jesus walked out to the disciples and Peter asked if he could walk on the water to Jesus. Peter did fine for a few steps, but then he took his eyes off Jesus and looked at the storm around him. He began to sink into the dark water and called out, "Lord, save me" (Matthew 14:30). That's the right response when we're in need, whether we need comfort in grief or courage in the face of fear. Jesus will help us when we call out to Him.

I heard about a little caravan of caterpillars who were crawling along the ground and crying because on their backs they were carrying the cocoon of one of their brothers. It was a funeral march, and they were sad because their caterpillar brother was gone.

But while this pitiful little scene was being played out on the earth, above the procession of caterpillars was a beautiful butterfly, wings glistening in the sunlight. This was the caterpillar they were mourning. He was not dead but alive, transformed and transfigured.

As we live and move along on earth, we have times of grief and sorrow. But we also need to remember to look up because above us stands the Son of God shining in all the splendor of heaven. Jesus is no longer in the form of a servant or dead on the cross but is alive and exalted. He is Lord, and because His name is exalted above every name, we who believe in Him and live by His name will be exalted with Him.

CHAPTER EIGHT

Muscular Christianity

If you can remember when Jack LaLanne first started leading exercises on television, I can almost guarantee you that you need to take a walk today to wake up those tired muscles!

LaLanne was a real pioneer in this field, but the fitness industry moved ahead at warp speed when the VCR made it possible for people to plug an exercise guru's video into their machine at home and follow along to get in shape. Now you can hardly flip through the channels without seeing at least half a dozen programs with people shadowboxing, dancing, stepping, rolling, lifting, climbing, or stretching. And if all of that looks too strenuous, you can buy the diet pills that burn fat while you sleep.

Home workout equipment has also improved over the years. Those early ones often looked like some kind of medieval torture device, but today you can get fit with nothing but a child's bounce ball that looks like it's on steroids. And I love the ads for fitness machines. While the camera pans the form of a man or woman with an incredibly sculpted physique, a voice says, "Get results like these in less than thirty minutes a day." The problem is that the guy on the screen is younger than some of the socks in my drawer.

Well, it doesn't matter whether you follow a workout session on television, hire a personal trainer at the gym, or exercise in a group for mutual encouragement. It doesn't matter how earnestly your exercise leader exhorts you to keep at it or introduces you to other people just like you who have gotten in shape. The fact is, getting fit is an intensely personal activity. No one can do it for you. I love what Christian comedienne Chonda Pierce says about her experience with a Jane Fonda workout video. Chonda said she plugged it in and sat on the couch watching it with a bag of Oreos yelling, "Knock yourself out, Jane!"

Beauty may only be skin-deep, but fat goes all the way to the bone. I don't know where you will be in your physical conditioning by the time you finish this book, but my hope and prayer is that it will help you avoid having a flabby faith.

I'm using the term *muscular Christianity* to describe a faith that is strong and dynamic, the kind of faith that gives us power with God and with people. I want to help believers develop a powerful faith that's going to impact the world and influence this culture for Christ. I fear that with all the resurgence of religion and Christianity in America, we would also have to admit that most people sitting in churches today are casual Christians, conventional Christians, and cultural Christians when God has called us to be muscular Christians.

If the church is going to be a force instead of a farce, we need to practice muscular Christianity. Philippians 2 gives us a spiritual workout that is failure-proof if we'll just follow it. Paul followed his great hymn of praise about Jesus in verses 5–11 with an intensely practical word of application: "Therefore, my beloved, as you have always obeyed, so now, not only as in my presence but much more in my absence, work out your own salvation with fear and trembling, for it is God who works in you, both to will and to work for his good pleasure" (vv. 12–13). Then in verses 14–17 he described several key elements in that process. We need to ask what it takes to develop a muscular Christianity.

WORK OUT YOUR FAITH

It's important to begin by talking about what the Bible does *not* say here. Paul didn't tell us to work *for* our salvation, which is a gift of grace we couldn't possibly earn. Rather, we are called to "work out" the salvation that God began working into our lives the day He saved us. In theological terms, this working out is our sanctification, the ongoing process by which we are to become more like Jesus Christ because we are sanctified or set apart for Him.

The difference between working to gain salvation and working to grow in the salvation that comes only through faith in Christ is as great as the gap between heaven and hell. If you are working out to get yourself in the best religious shape possible so you can stand before God and be approved, you are destined to be eternally disappointed.

God has freely given us everything in Jesus Christ. But that doesn't mean we can be spiritual couch potatoes who lounge our way to heaven. We need to work out what God has worked into us so that we become fully developed followers of Christ.

Whoever said that the Christian life was going to be easy anyway? Does anyone enlist in the military without expecting a disciplined regimen of exercise? In the same way, we are told, "Share in suffering as a good soldier of Christ Jesus" (2 Timothy 2:3).

I hope you noticed the words "your own salvation" in Philippians 2:12. Just as no one can exercise and get fit for you, no one can get saved or grow in Christ for you. You must have a salvation and a relationship with Christ that you can claim as your own.

I want to speak to men at this point because as a pastor I have seen so many men who are counting on their wives' faith rather than living their own. Their philosophy is, "I work and do the physical stuff around the house, and my wife takes care of the spiritual stuff with her and the kids. I don't get into that." The trouble is, that is not God's design for the home. Each of us has a personal responsibility before God.

Paul had a special relationship with the Christians at Philippi. They were his spiritual children; so it's understandable that they felt better when he was with them. But Paul was wise enough to know that the Philippians had to grow on their own, whether he was there or not. That's the reason for his plea to them to obey God whether he was present or absent.

Just like children with a loving parent, Christians can become overly attached to a particular leader. And who better to attach yourself to than the apostle Paul? But Paul wasn't building a personal following. He told the Corinthians:

And I, when I came to you, brothers, did not come proclaiming to you the testimony of God with lofty speech or wisdom. For I decided

to know nothing among you except Jesus Christ and him crucified . . .
that your faith might not rest in the wisdom of men but in the power
of God. *(1 Corinthians 2:1–5, emphasis added)*

Paul knew he was the messenger, not the message. One of his most
telling criticisms of the Judaizers who followed him around trying to
undo his work was that they weren't really interested in getting people
to obey the Law. They were just out to gain as many followers as possible so they could brag about it (Galatians 6:13).

We certainly need teachers and leaders, but the Bible tells us to fix or
fasten our eyes on Jesus (Hebrews 12:2). That's hard to do if we're following a human leader too intently. I thank God for the godly parents,
pastors, and teachers I had over the years. But the day came when I had
to learn to obey Christ and grow in Him without their oversight.

What would happen if you tried to run, lift weights, stretch, jump
rope, or do any other form of physical workout without a muscular
system? You wouldn't even be able to move, much less get in shape. God
has to put the muscles inside of you first.

What is true physically is even truer spiritually. Paul told the
Philippians they could work out their salvation because God had
worked salvation into them. Verse 13 of chapter 2 says that God both
"works in [us]" and enables us to accomplish that which pleases Him.

The Christian life isn't hard—it is *impossible* in our own strength.
We can't move from weakness to strength apart from the energizing
power of the Holy Spirit, who lives in us and works in us to do God's
will.

There's a wonderful balance to the Christian life. God will not do
for us what we are called to do, which is to work out our salvation by
disciplined spiritual exercise. And yet God never asks us to do anything
without supplying the power to do it. There's nothing more frustrat-
ing than to be told to do something you are incapable of doing. But
in Christ, we are capable of keeping God's commands because He is
the Enabler. And what is the power by which we live? Paul tells us in
Philippians 3:10: "the power of his [Christ's] resurrection." We talked
earlier about the awesome power it took to raise Jesus from the dead.

This same resurrection power is at work in you today! Paul's prayer for all believers included these words: "the immeasurable greatness of his power toward us who believe, according to the working of his great might that he worked in Christ when he raised him from the dead and seated him at his right hand in the heavenly places" (Ephesians 1:19–20). The word "power" here means "energy." I love to think of the energy of God working in my life. That's what makes the Christian life supernatural.

But why are we to work out our faith "with fear and trembling" (Philippians 2:12)? Not because we're afraid we're going to lose our salvation, but because we know that we are weak and vulnerable to the obstacles and temptations that the world, the flesh, and the devil put in our path. For the Christian, this fear is a holy respect for God and a wholesome awareness of our own human weakness.

That said, always remember these words: "I can do all things through him who strengthens me" (Philippians 4:13).

LIVE OUT YOUR FAITH

If you joined a fitness club and hired a trainer to help you get in shape, you'd be surprised and frustrated if that expert simply said, "OK, start working out and I'll watch," without any assessment of your needs or instruction on the equipment. A good physical trainer measures and weighs you, shows you how each piece of equipment operates and how to use it properly, and makes sure you're not over- or under-exerting yourself.

Paul was a good spiritual trainer. So when he told us, "Work out your own salvation," he didn't leave it at that. He followed up that exhortation with specific ways to help us get in shape as we seek to live out a muscular faith.

He began our workout in Philippians 2:14 by saying, "Do all things without *grumbling* or *questioning*" (emphasis added). These two words are very insightful, so we'll take some time on each one.

Another word for "grumbling" is "murmuring." Remember in school when you studied onomatopoeia? These are words such as *buzz* that sound like what they describe. *Murmur* is one of these words because even when you say it, you can feel the sense of something that is not overt but kind of an under-your-breath way of talking. Another good way to describe it is mumbling. Murmurers and mumblers are people who always seem to be unhappy about something and are always complaining and criticizing.

I heard about a man who was a chronic griper. He took his wife to a restaurant one night and started complaining as soon as they reached the parking lot. Nothing seemed to be right. He didn't like the parking, the waiter, or the menu. The table was in a bad location. It was too hot and then too cold in the building. The food took too long to arrive, and then it wasn't hot enough. And sure enough, his steak wasn't cooked right either. This went on during the entire meal.

As this couple was leaving, the waiter said to the man's wife, "I'm sorry your husband had such a miserable experience."

"Oh no," she responded, "he's perfectly happy because he got a chance to complain about everything."

Sad to say, the church of Jesus Christ is full of murmuring members. One pastor said, "I don't mind being swallowed by whales. I just don't like being nibbled to death by minnows."

A pastor friend received a note one Wednesday morning from a parishioner who among other charges accused him of not living what he preached. He put it in his pocket because it was too discouraging to deal with at the moment. That night he went to prayer meeting at the church, where a dear older woman came up to him and said, "Pastor, the Lord has given me a word for you. If God be for you, who can be against you?"

She said this not knowing about the accusing note my friend still had in his pocket. He ended the story by saying, "I get just enough Wednesday morning notes to keep me humble and just enough Wednesday evening notes to keep me from leaving the ministry."

Murmuring is a serious issue. That little bite of complaining here and nibble of criticism over there add up until they devour people. I'm telling you that as Christians we can't live like this. Here's what Paul said about the Israelites who grumbled all the way from Egypt to the edge of the Promised Land: "We must not . . . grumble, as some of them did and were destroyed by the Destroyer" (1 Corinthians 10:9–10). Take a few minutes sometime to read the story in Numbers 14:26–35, and you may be startled at the severity of God's judgment against those grumblers. Verse 34 says the people would find out what it was like to have God against them!

The reason for this is twofold: first, murmuring is a display of unbelief against God; and second, it sows discord and strife among His people. In the famous list of the seven things God hates (Proverbs 6:16–19), the seventh is "one who sows discord among brothers."

Now don't misunderstand. This does not mean we can never disagree on important matters. Unity does not require mere conformity for the sake of peace. But we can disagree agreeably without cannibalizing each other.

Have I convinced you to get on the workout machine and make sure you're toning up this area so you don't become a murmurer? I hope so. I don't know of any other place where the collective flabbiness of the body of Christ is more visible. Here's a good way to remember the attitude God wants us to have: determine to be humbly grateful instead of grumbly hateful.

The second word in Philippians 2:14 is "questioning," which can also mean "to argue." This word may surprise you because it's the Greek word for "dialogue." The verse could be translated, "Do everything without dialoguing."

You may wonder what's wrong with that. After all, *dialogue* is one of the most popular buzzwords of our age. It sounds so positive. The liberal church says we need to dialogue with other faiths so we don't become too exclusionary by insisting that Jesus Christ is the only way to heaven. Of course, what they usually mean by that is talking *ad nauseam* without ever taking a stand on important doctrinal issues.

The context of Philippians 2 suggests the argumentative side of this word. It refers to people who are always looking for a verbal fight. They love to argue. And more often than not, they're the kind of people who wouldn't believe something if an angel from heaven came down and told them it was so.

I'm convinced that countless marriages, to say nothing of countless churches, would be transformed if God's people would start blessing each other instead of blasting each other. It's interesting that one quality of true *agape* love is that it "believes all things" (1 Corinthians 13:7). We're not talking about being gullible, but merciful. Love believes the best about our spouses, our children, our spiritual leaders, and others. Love not only believes the best, but it looks for and expects the best from others. But chronic debaters look for and expect the worst because they love to fight.

This workout is getting pretty intense, but we are not done. We are also to be "blameless and innocent, children of God without blemish in the midst of a crooked and twisted generation, among whom you shine as lights in the world" (Philippians 2:15).

The contrasts here could be not any stronger. Our world is a depraved, perverse place. People's minds have become so twisted by impurity and immorality.

Our job is not to hide from the culture but to live "blameless" lives in the middle of it. This word doesn't mean sinless but authentic. We're to be real and genuine. Everyone fails, but people will respect you if you're genuine. One big turnoff for people outside the church is those inside who say one thing and do another—hypocrites who wear a mask, pretending to be someone they're not.

The word "innocent" refers to purity. I love this definition: "inexperienced with evil." There ought to be a certain naiveté about a believer when it comes to the filth in our world. We know way too much about things we ought not to know about at all.

It's easy to blame Hollywood and other popular media for this—and to be sure, life would be a lot more wholesome if we didn't have television shows about sexual predators and the lives of drugged-out rock stars and divas. But televisions still come equipped with an Off button.

I'm not advocating a "hear no evil, see no evil" approach to life. But what Paul is talking about here is an unhealthy familiarity with evil that dims the light of our witness and allows us to get so accustomed to the dark that we can't see things as clearly as we ought. This is called compromise.

Have you ever walked out of a blazing noonday sun into a dark restaurant? You can't see a thing for a minute or two until your eyes adjust to the darkness. And what happens when you go outside again after an hour or so in the restaurant? The same thing in reverse; you can hardly see. The bright light actually hurts your eyes until they readjust to it.

Some people wonder how we as Christians can be pure and innocent in this world. It just seems unreasonable to them for God to expect so much when evil is so pervasive. But remember, God provides the ability to keep His commands. He is at work in us "both to will and to work for his good pleasure." The "will" has to do with our desire and determination to obey. Raise your standards, and then stretch to reach them in the strength God gives you.

GIVE OUT YOUR FAITH

The next phrase in Philippians 2 packs a lot of meaning into a few words. We are to live "holding fast to the word of life" (v. 16). When you hold fast to something, you clutch it close to your heart, and you don't let go when someone tries to take it from you. This is why we need a muscular faith. If you've ever tried to take something from a strong person who doesn't want to give it up, you understand the meaning of "holding fast."

Paul told Timothy, "Guard the good deposit entrusted to you" (2 Timothy 1:14). This "deposit" is the same as "the word of life." It's the gospel of Jesus Christ. We hold tightly to the gospel that has been once for all delivered to the church when we defend the truth of Christ against the false gospels and distortions that people bring against the Word of God.

But while the gospel is to be guarded, it isn't to be hoarded. We're to give the message out. That's part of what it means to hold it fast. The picture I like is that of a runner in a relay race. He has to have a firm grip on the baton as he runs his leg of the race, but he also has to hand it carefully to the next runner or the baton falls and the race is lost.

All of us are called to share our faith, to shine as lights in a dark world. People everywhere are desperately looking for real life. Not just existence, but a life that's worth living. We have the message of abundant and eternal life in Jesus Christ, and we need to give it out.

You Can Share Your Faith Using a Simple and Clear Gospel Presentation

(The following paragraphs have been adapted from Dr. Ken Hemphill and Frank Harber's evangelism tool *Got Life?* See "Got Life!" by Adam Myrick, in *Journal of the Southern Baptist Convention*, June-July 2007; www.sbclife.org/Articles/2000/09/Sla8.asp.)

The message of the gospel is about life. So I want to give you a simple and clear tool you can use to present the gospel to anybody. It follows the acrostic L-I-F-E.

- Love
- Isolated
- Faith
- Eternal Life

First, God **loves** you and has a wonderful plan for your life. John 3:16 is still the best news anyone will ever hear: "For God so loved the world, that he gave his only Son, that whoever believes in him should not perish but have eternal life."

There is not a person on the face of the earth whom God does not love. That's why we want to give out the gospel through missions and through the media, but also person-to-person as neighbor tells neighbor and friend tells friend that God loves them.

But there is a problem, because we are **isolated** or separated from God by our sin. The prophet Isaiah said:

Behold, the LORD's hand is not shortened, that it cannot save, or his ear dull, that it cannot hear; but your iniquities have made a separation between you and your God, and your sins have hidden his face from you so that he does not hear. (Isaiah 59:1–2)

There is also not a person on earth who is not separated from God by sin. The Bible says, "None is righteous, no, not one" (Romans 3:10), and "All have sinned and fall short of the glory of God" (Romans 3:23).

Every person lives in isolation from God and from others. Relationships are torn apart, families are destroyed, and lives are broken because of sin and the spirit of independence that says to God, "I don't need You." But the problem is, sin leads to permanent isolation from God if it is not forgiven. "The wages of sin is death" (Romans 6:23).

But you can be forgiven of your sins by putting your **faith** in the Lord Jesus Christ who died on the cross for your sins and who was raised on the third day to guarantee you eternal life. If you will turn from your sins and trust in Jesus Christ, no longer trusting in yourself and your good deeds to make you acceptable to God, you will be saved. The Bible says, "For by grace you have been saved through faith. And this is not your own doing; it is the gift of God, not a result of works, so that no one may boast" (Ephesians 2:8–9).

And when you reach out to God in faith, He gives you the gift of **eternal life**, which begins the moment you receive Jesus Christ. We read this promise in God's Word: "I write these things to you who believe in the name of the Son of God that you may know that you have eternal life" (1 John 5:13).

You can use this **L-I-F-E** gospel presentation anywhere, spelling it out on a napkin at a restaurant or just in conversation. Let's give out our faith and see our friends and loved ones come to experience eternal life in Jesus Christ.

You Can Take Advantage of Some Incredible Tools for Sharing Christ

I am a big believer in gospel tracts and booklets. They are easy to carry, attractive, interesting to hand out, and ready to be read whenever the recipient opens them. They are also tools that anyone can use effectively. Tracts are a tremendous way to give out your faith. My publisher, Crossway Books, is a division of a ministry called Good News Publishers that has been producing gospel tracts since 1938.

The best argument I know of for tracts is a friend of mine in South Florida, a Jewish man whose life got messed up in the sixties. He was separated from his wife and was just bumming around the country when he stopped at a gas station in the Carolinas and found half of a gospel tract on the ground. He picked it up, read it, and got interested. So he asked if there was anybody in that town who could tell him the rest of the story.

Somebody told him about a woman who was known for her witness for Jesus Christ. My friend knocked on her door and told her about finding the tract, and she led him to faith in Christ. Today he is a minister of the gospel of Christ, a Messianic Jew who has a pastoral counseling ministry in Florida—all because of a tract. The Word of God is alive, even when it's lying on the ground at a gas station. There are many more people out there like my friend; so let's keep giving out the gospel in every way we can.

POUR OUT YOUR FAITH

Paul told the Philippians, "Even if I am to be poured out as a drink offering upon the sacrificial offering of your faith, I am glad and rejoice with you all" (Philippians 2:17).

This is a reference to the drink offering that was part of Israel's worship. An early example is Jacob as he left his place of exile with his family and possessions to go back to Canaan and face his brother Esau. God appeared to Jacob and assured him of His promises, and in response Jacob worshiped: "Jacob set up a pillar in the place where he had spoken with him, a pillar of stone. He poured out a drink offering and poured oil on it" (Genesis 35:14).

Becoming a drink offering may sound rather tame, but it was another metaphor for death. The best example is Psalm 22:14, a prophecy of Jesus' crucifixion, where the psalmist wrote, "I am poured out like water, and all my bones are out of joint."

Paul felt that his life was coming to an end, but that was fine with him because he knew he had given his life in service to Christ on behalf of believers like those at Philippi. Besides, Paul knew that "to live is Christ, and to die is gain" (Philippians 1:21).

Paul was happy to stay and serve Christ or to go and be with Him. Either way, the apostle was determined that the last drop of life in him was going to be poured out for Jesus Christ. That's what I want to do. I don't want to just spend my days turning the pages of a calendar.

I read about a woman who wrote to an advice columnist. This woman had always wanted to go to college, but she was now thirty-six years old and felt it was too late to realize her dream. "If I take four years to go to college now," she wrote, "I'll be forty by the time I graduate."

The columnist responded very wisely, "How old will you be in four years if you don't go to college?"

So if you want to be fit for life, work out. Be strong in the Lord and the power of His might. Be a muscular Christian.

CHAPTER NINE

A Band of Brothers and Sisters

Robert Fulghum is a writer who became famous for his essay, "All I Really Need to Know I Learned in Kindergarten." Fulghum's collection of essays by that name stayed on the *New York Times* bestseller list for nearly two years in the mid-eighties.

One piece of advice from that essay about the important lessons in life is that when we go outside, "It's still a good idea to hold hands and stick together," just as we were taught to do as little children.

But the fact is that kindergarten teachers weren't the first to realize our need for relationships. God made us to need and to seek companionship with others. We have the perfect example of this in the fellowship of the Godhead—Father, Son, and Spirit in eternal relationship. And illustrations of our need and desire for relationships are all around us.

I'm sure you've had the experience of attending a play or a concert with a group of strangers called an audience. What often happens is that you all get so caught up in the moment that you find yourself laughing, sharing stories, or singing along with the people around you as if you were old friends on a night out together. And depending on the event, you may even wind up standing and holding hands across the aisle to sing a song together. Even working out is more enjoyable if you have someone with whom to jog, walk, or lift.

My title for this chapter comes from the acclaimed television mini-series *Band of Brothers*, about an amazing army unit in World War II.

Those men were comrades in every sense of the word. The old saying is that there are no atheists in foxholes. Judging by what soldiers tell us about the demands and dangers of war, there aren't too many soldiers who want to be alone in a foxhole, period.

Paul wasn't in a foxhole when he wrote the book of Philippians. That would have been an upgrade from his living conditions in a Roman dungeon. He must have felt alone at times, and later in what we believe was his final imprisonment before his execution the great apostle expressed a very tender need for the companionship of Timothy, his beloved son in the faith: "Do your best to come to me soon" (2 Timothy 4:9).

Timothy was part of Paul's band of brothers about whom he wrote in Philippians 2:19–30. Timothy and Epaphroditus, who was a member of the Philippian church and a dear brother to Paul, exemplify what it means to have a band of brothers, or sisters, in the family of faith who are vital to our spiritual well-being and our overall health. I know many people have somewhat of an independent streak, but how lonely and empty life would be without people who add fullness and freshness to our lives.

When God wanted to reach out and bring the world to Himself, He did it by sending a Savior/Friend who "sticks closer than a brother" (Proverbs 18:24). His name is Jesus, and because we are related to Him by faith, the Bible says that He "is not ashamed to call [us] brothers" (Hebrews 2:11).

What a phenomenal thought that Jesus is eager to claim us as family! I'm reminded of the time in Jesus' ministry when it was reported to Him that His mother and brothers wanted to see Him. Jesus looked at His disciples gathered around Him and said, "Here are my mother and my brothers! For whoever does the will of God, he is my brother and sister and mother" (Mark 3:34–35). It is also sobering to remember that even Jesus, the Son of God, did not want to be alone during His agony in the Garden of Gethsemane but took His three closest disciples with Him and asked them to support Him in prayer (Matthew 26:36–38).

That is the way God made us. So it shouldn't surprise us that Paul, the greatest Christian who ever lived in my estimation, the apostle of the Christian faith and a powerful missionary of the gospel, sought out relationships and vitally connected brothers and sisters in Christ who served with him. He was always sending greetings to friends in the churches to which he wrote, the best example being all the people he mentioned in Romans 16.

In Philippians 2 we see two members of Paul's band of brothers who helped him turn the world upside down. Paul joined with Timothy and Epaphroditus to form a powerful trio in Philippi. The Scripture says concerning the blessing of having friends, "A threefold cord is not quickly broken" (Ecclesiastes 4:12). Paul was the focused leader, Timothy the faithful minister, and Epaphroditus the fearless risk-taker. As we look at each of these men and see how their lives connected, we'll discover how God uses people like you and me today to accomplish His work, regardless of our personalities and gifts.

EVERY BAND OF BROTHERS OR SISTERS NEEDS A FOCUSED, COMMITTED LEADER

The one thing we can say about Paul is that after he met Jesus Christ on the road to Damascus, he became totally committed and absolutely focused on the goal of knowing Christ and making Him known. Paul only had one item on his spiritual "to do" list: "One thing I do: forgetting what lies behind and straining forward to what lies ahead, I press on toward the goal for the prize of the upward call of God in Christ Jesus" (Philippians 3:14).

The explanation for Paul's all-out commitment is found in the answers he got to two key questions he asked Jesus as he lay facedown in the dust outside Damascus, blinded by the light from heaven. The first question Paul asked was, "Who are you, Lord?" (Acts 9:5). And when Jesus answered, "I am Jesus, whom you are persecuting," Paul's next question was, "What shall I do, Lord?" You won't find this question in Acts 9, but this is what Paul himself said he asked when he later recounted this experience to the crowd in Jerusalem (Acts 22:10).

The answer to this question came to Paul via Ananias, when Jesus told this Christian brother in Damascus to go to Paul (who was still called Saul) with this message: "He is a chosen instrument of mine to carry my name before the Gentiles and kings and the children of Israel. For I will show him how much he must suffer for the sake of my name" (Acts 9:15–16).

Now there's a calling that will focus your life in a hurry! Once you discover who Jesus is and what He wants you to do, you have the basic tools you need to be fit for life. When it's all said and done, what will matter most is that we know Christ and are making Him known to the world around us.

Paul never blinked at his calling, and now here he was years later in Philippi with his life being poured out like a drink offering (Philippians 2:17). But we just can't get away from the fact that he was filled with joy—certainly not because of his circumstances, but because he knew he had been faithful to Christ and Christ had been more than faithful to him. A big part of Paul's joy was also found in his relationships with his brothers and sisters in the gospel.

Someone may say, "Well, I'm no Paul. Can God use me?" Yes, He can, because every Paul needs a Timothy, a man who didn't have Paul's powerful personality but who served faithfully with him.

EVERY BAND OF BROTHERS OR SISTERS NEEDS A FAITHFUL MINISTER

I earlier referred to Timothy as a faithful minister. He became a ministry companion of Paul's on the apostle's second missionary journey that took him into Greece and specifically to Philippi. Timothy was from Lystra, where Paul met him, heard the good reports of Timothy from his "brothers" (interesting), and learned of his godly mother and grandmother, Eunice and Lois (Acts 16:1–5; see 2 Timothy 1:5).

Timothy was the son of a Gentile who was probably an unbeliever; so we can understand from this alone how Paul would become like a father to him. Timothy is identified with Paul more than is any other person in the New Testament. We find out why in Philippians 2. Paul wrote concerning Timothy: "I have no one like him, who will be genuinely concerned for your welfare. They all seek their own interests, not those of Jesus Christ. But you know Timothy's proven worth, how as a son with a father he has served with me in the gospel" (2:20–22).

Imagine the doors that would open to you if someone of Paul's stature wrote a letter like that to your prospective employer as a job reference! This reminds me of a great story about Horace Greeley, the famous newspaper editor who said, "Go west, young man, go west."

Greeley's handwriting was so notoriously poor that no one could read it. One day he wrote a note to an employee, telling the man he was being fired for gross neglect of his duties. When Greeley saw the man several years later, the former employee expressed his gratitude to the puzzled Greeley. The man explained that since no one could read Greeley's writing, he used the note as a letter of recommendation from the great Horace Greeley and got several good jobs with it.

Well, no such problem existed between Paul and Timothy. There was no mistaking Paul's confidence in and affection for Timothy. The phrase "like him" is much richer in the original language. It means someone who is "like-minded" or, even better, "one-souled" with another. Paul and Timothy were soul mates.

We usually hear that word used of married couples, and a husband and wife certainly need to be soul mates as well as house- and bedmates. I tell young couples who come to me to be married that they need to be friends as well as lovers—not only in love, but in "like." I think you know what I mean, even if you're not married.

Someone has said that while it may be possible to divorce your spouse, it's impossible to divorce your best friend. Deb Graham is my dearest friend on earth—the person above all others I want to spend time with—as well as my wife and the love of my life. I'm so grateful for that compatibility.

Faithful Brothers and Sisters Have Certain Important Qualities

That's the kind of one-soul relationship we also need to develop with a handful of friends who are our band of brothers or sisters in Christ. One great quality about Timothy as a disciple was that he was *teachable*. Are you teachable? Don't think this is only a trait for followers and disciples. I believe Paul was the most teachable person on earth. He said to the Philippians in chapter 3, "Not that I have already obtained this or am already perfect . . ." (v. 12).

Timothy was *available* as well. If you trace the occurrences of Timothy's name through the New Testament, you'll find that in most cases he was carrying out some critical ministry task for Paul.

Timothy was also *accountable* to Paul and to the church. Friends in the body of Christ hold each other accountable. One of the great things about having a band of Christian brothers like Paul, Timothy, and Epaphroditus is that they keep each other accountable, and they are there for each other when one is in trouble, needs encouragement in their life and service for Christ, or have fallen and need to be restored.

If you're not a Paul, pray for a godly older person who can be a mentor and older brother or sister to you. The person doesn't even have to be older in years but may just be older and more seasoned in the faith. Timothy relied on the teaching, guidance, and encouragement of Paul to carry out his ministry, especially when Paul left Timothy in the large and spiritually intimidating city of Ephesus to pastor the church there. That's what the books of 1 and 2 Timothy are all about.

I read a story about two buddies in World War I who were raised together, enlisted together, trained together, shipped out together, and fought side by side in Europe. One day one of the men was mortally wounded as he left their foxhole to take up another position. His buddy in the foxhole decided to go get him despite heavy fire from the enemy.

But as the second man crawled to his friend, he was also seriously wounded. After ministering to his dying buddy right to the end, he somehow managed to make it back to his lines. His sergeant saw the severity of the man's wounds and realized he would also die. So the sergeant asked him, "Why did you do that? Your buddy wasn't going to live, and now I'm going to lose two men. Was it worth it?"

That soldier looked up at his sergeant and said, "Yes, it was, because the last thing he said to me was, 'Jim, I knew you'd come. I knew you'd come.'"

Do your friends say that about you? Do they know you'll always be available? Paul made an amazing statement about his band of brothers and sisters in Galatia: "I testify to you that, if possible, you would have gouged out your eyes and given them to me" (Galatians 4:15).

EVERY BAND OF BROTHERS OR SISTERS NEEDS A FEARLESS RISK-TAKER

The third person in this band of brothers is Epaphroditus. Paul was the focused leader, Timothy was the faithful minister, and Epaphroditus was the fearless risk-taker. His name means "charming," "lovely," or "favored." Paul said he was worthy of honor. I want you to see Epaphroditus's story in full:

> *I have thought it necessary to send to you Epaphroditus my brother and fellow worker and fellow soldier, and your messenger and minister to my need, for he has been longing for you all and has been distressed because you heard that he was ill. Indeed he was ill, near to death. But God had mercy on him, and not only on him but on me also, lest I should have sorrow upon sorrow. I am the more eager to send him, therefore, that you may rejoice at seeing him again, and that I may be less anxious. So receive him in the Lord with all joy, and honor such men, for he nearly died for the work of Christ,* risking his life *to complete what was lacking in your service to me. (Philippians 2:25–30, emphasis added)*

Epaphroditus was a valued and respected member of the church at Philippi who was entrusted to deliver the church's package of supplies to Paul in Rome, where he was under arrest. Paul said in his letter, "I am well supplied, having received from Epaphroditus the gifts you sent" (Philippians 4:18).

But as a result of this mission for Christ and the church and his friend Paul, Epaphroditus became seriously ill and nearly died. We don't know what hardships he encountered on the way or the state of his health before he made the trip, but Epaphroditus was a risk-taker who refused to play it safe. Compared to other people in Scripture, Epaphroditus was a relative unknown. His name is only mentioned twice in the Bible, in Philippians 2:25 and 4:18. But Paul gave his friend very high marks.

We Need to Be Brothers-in-Arms with Our Fellow Christians

Paul referred to Epaphroditus as a "brother" (Philippians 2:25). This word of comradeship meant a lot in the Greco-Roman world of that day. The culture in which Paul and Epaphroditus lived was deeply polarized politically, spiritually, and culturally between Greeks and Romans, Jews and Gentiles, the rich and the poor, the slaves and the free. There was virtually no middle class.

This is one reason the gospel was such a radical and countercultural message. In Christ, diverse people were brought together as one and were taught to treat each other as brothers and sisters in a family. No one had ever heard of such a thing. The early church had slaves and wealthy slave owners meeting together.

Things really haven't changed that much today. In America we have red states and blue states, and people are deeply divided over issues of class, race, culture, and religion. There are a lot of songs about the value of love and how people need to come together. But today, as in Paul's day, the only real unity that will last is when men and women put their faith in Christ and become bands of brothers and sisters in Him.

My prayer for the church is for believers in Jesus Christ to become truly knitted together and like-minded as soul mates in Christ. Epaphroditus stands out as an example of what Jesus meant when He said, "Greater love has no one than this, that someone lays down his life for his friends" (John 15:13).

We Need to Be Workers Alongside Our Fellow Christians

Paul also referred to Epaphroditus as a "fellow worker" (Philippians 2:25). Many people want to be in the family of faith—they just don't want to do any work. These are people who, as someone has said, want to serve God, but only in an advisory capacity. They're like the lazy brother-in-law whom comedians make jokes about, except that there's nothing funny about people in the body of Christ who refuse to work. The problem of freeloaders got so bad in the church at Thessalonica that Paul told them to shun the lazy person (2 Thessalonians 3:6) and issued this order: "If anyone is not willing to work, let him not eat" (v. 10).

One thing is sure—Epaphroditus would not have gone hungry. One of the fastest ways to find true friends and spiritual soul mates, to say nothing of growing in your faith, is to get busy serving and working in your church. It is when we get side-by-side serving Christ with others that we see their hearts and draw close to them. I guarantee you that when you get together with going and growing Christians, you will grow, and the family of God will build true unity.

But too many people today look at the church as sort of a religious mall, so they approach it as a consumer. They look over the ministry opportunities to see what looks interesting or inviting, but not too demanding. They may try one or two things to see how they fit, but if it feels too uncomfortable they give it up. They're like the lazy brother-in-law in a popular movie comedy who couldn't seem to find a job. When the main character questioned him on it, he said, "I'm waiting for something to open up in middle management."

The church has sung "Standing on the Promises" for many years, but too many saints are sitting on the premises. I can testify from experience that it doesn't matter what size a church is or how many people attend. There is still that faithful band of brothers and sisters like Epaphroditus who are carrying a disproportionate share of the workload. Many of them need some R&R, but there's no one to step in.

Epaphroditus had the heart of a servant. We don't know very much about him, but what we know is good. He wasn't a Paul or even a Timothy. He was just a package carrier for Christ. He delivered the church's care package to Paul, which no doubt included money as well as other things. Of course, Epaphroditus must have been trustworthy to be selected to handle these funds with complete faithfulness.

Some Christians aren't waiting for something to open up in middle management before they become workers in the church. They just believe God can't use them because of something in their past. Well, few people in the church today have this sordid background: "I was a blasphemer, persecutor, and insolent opponent" (1 Timothy 1:13); "Christ Jesus came into the world to save sinners, of whom I am the foremost" (v. 15). Add prison time to that list, and your church would have quite a character on its hands. But you'd also have the apostle Paul.

It's amazing to realize Paul probably wouldn't pass the criminal background check that churches have to do on many workers. I'm certainly not advocating hiring people who fail the test. I'm just saying that God can use imperfect people who are still in process as His workers. Epaphroditus was a worker.

We Need to Serve as Soldiers Alongside Our Fellow Christians

Epaphroditus was also a "fellow soldier" (Philippians 2:25) who didn't fail to show up for duty. A soldier is under authority and does what he's told. We're under the authority of our Commander-in-Chief, the Lord Jesus Christ, and must do what He says. And just as soldiers meet opposition when they try to advance, so do we as soldiers of Christ.

There is opposition in the culture to the message that we bring, but we need to be soldiers for Christ, earnestly contending for the faith (Jude 3), fighting the good fight of faith (2 Timothy 4:7). The French Foreign Legion used a motto years ago that has been adopted by other military organizations: "If I falter, push me. If I stumble, pick me up. If I retreat, shoot me."

It's a good thing the church doesn't shoot its retreating soldiers. Too many believers are running in full retreat from the enemy because the battle is too intense. But there's only one place for a soldier of Christ to go—forward. In one sense the church is like the staging ground for its forces, the command center where we gather to get our orders and be supplied so we can go out and engage the enemy.

We have no reason to retreat because the victory is already ours in Christ Jesus. No other commander in history has been able to say, "You're going into a real battle, but don't be afraid. I have overcome the enemy." But that's exactly what Jesus said in John 16:33: "Take heart; I have overcome the world." I like what one guy said: "When I leave my church, I'm ready to charge hell with a water pistol."

We Need to Serve the Lord Alongside Our Fellow Servants

Paul used two other words to describe Epaphroditus: "minister" and "messenger." We saw that his messenger duties included traveling between Paul in Rome and the church in Philippi. As a minister, Epaphroditus tended to Paul's needs even though he nearly lost his life doing so. That's what brothers and sisters in the body of Christ do for each other. We're not to hide in our foxhole while our buddy is wounded and needs help.

We need more risk-takers in the work of Christ. Too often churches are led by undertakers or caretakers instead of risk-takers. I want to be a risk-taker. I want our church to do whatever it takes in our generation for the sake of the gospel.

The word *minister* is often used of ordained professionals in the church. But the word simply means "servant." All of us can be servants because there are only four abilities needed to serve Christ: availability, expendability, reliability, and responsibility. Epaphroditus had these qualities, and Paul said we ought to honor people like him.

Paul, Timothy, and Epaphroditus were a great band of brothers for Jesus Christ. God help us to be like them.

CHAPTER TEN

Keeping It Real

Maybe I shouldn't admit it, but I watch the TV program *American Idol*. For me the main entertainment is what the three judges are going to say to a contestant. One of the judges, Randy, may say something negative to a performer and then add, "Just keeping it real, dog, just keeping it real."

I like the idea of keeping it real, and I think Paul would too. The book of Philippians is all about how to have real faith in Jesus Christ and experience genuine joy and authentic happiness.

THE ROAD TO HAPPINESS

Words, like people, have a way of changing as they get older. The word *happiness* is a good example. When our founders wrote in the Declaration of Independence that God endowed us with a right to "the pursuit of happiness," they were not using that word the way it is used today. To the founders, happiness referred more to the common good of the people—happiness in the sense of having the things that are needful and being able to live and worship free of oppression and fear. In those days the idea of happiness had a certain nobility and honor to it.

But today the mantra in America is, "Do whatever makes you happy," which being interpreted means that it doesn't matter if something is illegal, immoral, or fattening. If doing it or smoking it or sniffing it makes somebody happy, that's cool because making ourselves happy and trying to eliminate all discomfort is the highest good.

However we define happiness, we've been pursuing it in this country for over 230 years now. That's a lot of pursuing, so how are we doing? On the surface, pretty well. We're the most prosperous nation in history, and we have more amusements and comfort devices than anyone ever dreamed could exist.

Relationships Are Falling Apart at an Alarming Rate

But since we're keeping it real, let's dig a little deeper and see how we're really doing. Marriages and families are breaking apart at an unprecedented rate. So many people are unhappy, isolated, and angry in the home, the workplace, and at school that names like Columbine and Virginia Tech are now part of our national history. And depression is no longer the family secret to be talked about in hushed tones. It seems to be the new national malady. In 1992 twelve million prescriptions were written for antidepressants in America. In 2005 that number climbed to 157 million prescriptions, including eleven million antidepressant prescriptions for children under twelve years of age. Teen suicides are also occurring in epidemic proportions.

Since the theme of this book is fitness, it's also worth pointing out that more Americans are unhappy with their bodies than ever before, at least judging by the incredibly large and growing industry of cosmetic plastic surgery and body sculpting. Even much of the fitness industry that focuses on worthy goals such as physical conditioning and correct dieting seems to be driven by a marketing frenzy that turns a lot of people into fitness fanatics.

I'm certainly not being critical of those who struggle with mental illness. And I wouldn't discourage anyone who wants to get in better shape. I'm just asking, are we really happy? And if not, why not?

Several Factors Are Fueling This Epidemic of Unhappiness

I believe the epidemic of unhappiness in this country can be tied to several factors. One is values that are badly misplaced and misdirected. What happens when you start out with the wrong objective or destination in front of you or the wrong map to the right destination? You can't help but wind up in the wrong place. That's what many people are doing today in their pursuit of happiness. They're seeking it in all the wrong places and down all the wrong roads. They're like the driver barreling along the road when his wife said, "Honey, aren't we lost?"

"Yeah," her husband answered, "but we're making great time!"

A lot of people are going fast and making time, but they're headed the wrong way. And when they come to the dead-end, they wonder what happened.

A second factor that I believe fuels a lot of the unhappiness around us is the mistaken idea that true happiness is dependent on our circumstances and experiences in life. This formula says that you can only be happy when good and pleasant things happen to you. The corollary of this is that it is impossible for you to be happy when painful and unpleasant things happen to you. But you don't have to know the Bible to know that this approach to life doesn't square with reality. If it did, Hollywood would be the happiest place on earth.

Life is a little bit like the game of golf. I remember one day when I really had it going. After six holes I was doing so well I thought I had finally arrived and was ready for the PGA Tour. But my euphoria evaporated on the seventh hole as my swing suddenly went south and the ball started going north, south, east, and west. On the first six holes I looked like Ben Hogan. But on the next six holes I looked more like Hulk Hogan hacking and chopping away. And in the process my golf-induced happiness evaporated as fast as my good stroke.

Many people's entire outlook on life rises and falls on circumstances. Being good Americans, we figure that if our team, our job, our house, or even our spouse is the cause of our unhappiness, it's time to get a new one. We're like the guy who said of his marriage, "I thought I was marrying the ideal, but I got a raw deal, and now I want a new deal." Others decide that happiness is waiting for them in the newest piece of technology or the latest machine to make life easier.

Happiness Is Not Found in Chasing the Wind

All of this is what the wisest man who ever lived called "vanity and a striving after wind" (Ecclesiastes 1:14). Have you ever chased the wind? A friend who lives in the country where the wind blows all the time had a gust of wind blow his mail out of his hand one day as he was walking back to the house. He said he ran through his half-acre front yard looking like a drunken tap dancer, trying to chase down the pieces of mail and step on them before the wind blew them another twenty feet away.

That's how some people chase after happiness and contentment in life. About the time they think they have it, the winds of life seem to blow it a little farther out of reach. And what may even be sadder, a lot of the stuff that people rely on for their joy isn't all that satisfying when they finally get it. It's like cotton candy that is sweet to the taste for a few seconds and then dissolves into nothing.

WE MUST RECEIVE THE JOY-GIVER WHO WANTS TO FILL OUR LIVES

One of the secrets to life is not only knowing the right questions to ask, but knowing the right *person* to ask. If someone were to ask where true happiness in life is to be found, I would point them to the apostle Paul and his statement that opens the third chapter of Philippians: "Finally, my brothers, rejoice in the Lord." He said it again even more forcefully later in Philippians 4:4: "Rejoice in the Lord always; again I will say, Rejoice."

Paul was the right person to ask because his focus was on Jesus Christ and not on the stuff of earth, and because he was in circumstances that most people would consider to be the least likely to produce any kind of happiness or joy. Paul may have been confined in his body, but his chains could not imprison his spirit. He was free in Christ and full of Christ, and so he could rejoice even in prison.

I wonder if as this letter was being read to the Philippian church, someone raised his or her hand and said, "Wait a minute. How could Paul be so positive with all that he's suffering? Is this real?"

And then I imagine a booming voice in the back: "Oh yes, Paul's joy is for real. Let me tell you what I saw. You know that I was a jailer at the local prison when Paul and Silas were brought in one night after being savagely beaten by the authorities. I was ordered to put their feet in stocks and show them no mercy. I locked them up and went back to my post.

"But then I heard something I had never heard in that jail before— singing. Paul and Silas were singing at the top of their lungs, joyful songs of praise to Jesus. I just dismissed them as religious fanatics, but about midnight there was a terrible shaking. I realized it was an earthquake and ran to the cells. The doors were open, and I thought the prisoners had escaped, so I was ready to kill myself.

"But Paul called out, 'Don't do that. We're all here.' I ran in and fell at his feet. I was shaking so hard, all I could say was, 'What must I do to be saved?' Paul told me about Jesus, and I and my family were saved that night. Now we sing the same songs of praise to Jesus Christ that Paul sang. Let me tell you, Paul and his joy are for real."

I think many of us have the idea that being a joyful, singing Christian is only for extroverts. But the joy available to us in Christ has nothing to do with personality type or temperaments. We are all called to experience outrageous, contagious joy in Christ.

Too many Christians are joyless. Satan often attacks us at this very point and tries to steal our joy. But real joy is not in things or other people or circumstances. Rather, "The joy of the LORD is your strength" (Nehemiah 8:10).

If the Bible commands us to be joyful in the Lord, that means it is something we can do. Joy is not a response tied to emotions that are beyond our control. In fact, joy is more of an attitude of the mind than a product of the emotions. We can see that in Philippians 4:8, where the Bible tells us to adopt a new way of thinking: "Whatever is true, whatever is honorable, whatever is just, whatever is pure, whatever is lovely, whatever is commendable, if there is any excellence, if there is anything worthy of praise, think about these things."

How we think determines the direction and even the destiny of our lives. Someone may say, "Oh, I get it. You're talking about that mind over matter thing, positive thinking." Well, it's true that positive thinking beats negative thinking every time. But what I'm talking about is Christ-centered thinking rooted in His Word instead of circumstance-driven thinking rooted in what may happen tomorrow to change our mood.

The Bible says, "A joyful heart is good medicine, but a crushed spirit dries up the bones" (Proverbs 17:22). I could quote pages of medical studies that show that happy, optimistic, upbeat people have lower levels of stress hormones, while others are assaulted by a whole range of negative factors that can attack the immune system and other parts of the body. We've all heard about the medicinal benefits of laughter.

Again, I'm not just talking about putting on a happy face even when you don't feel like it. Philippians 4:8 is a constant reminder that we can know real joy every day because real happiness is a choice. To focus our minds and hearts on what we believe is sound advice. For example, in Psalm 119:111 the psalmist wrote, "Your testimonies are my heritage forever, for they are the joy of my heart." If you want joy, then fill your life with God's Word.

Happiness Is Not Found in Being Problem-Free

Two of the best reasons for focusing our minds on God and His Word are found in Philippians itself: "I can do all things through him who strengthens me" (4:13), and "My God will supply every need of yours according to his riches in glory in Christ Jesus" (4:19).

I don't know your circumstances, but I can guarantee you from personal experience and the testimony of many other believers that if these two promises are implanted on your heart and mind, you will live a joyful life. And amazingly, it's in the heat of adversity that the joy of Christ can be most powerful as the Holy Spirit strengthens you.

Problems and pain are facts of life for all of us. No one's going to deny that Christians suffer the same problems as anyone else. The difference is that our trials have a purpose. God is working in our lives—creatively, constantly, constructively. This means we can rejoice even in the most rigorous difficulties. "Count it all joy, my brothers, when you meet trials of various kinds" (James 1:2).

We Have Good Reasons to Be Joyful

Let's add up the reasons we can rejoice in the Lord. First, God is sovereign over all the trials and situations of our lives. He's in control; so we can be sure that our lives are not accidents waiting to happen. Every parent has had the experience of turning away from a small child for just a second or two, only to turn back and find that in that instant the little one has disappeared. When we lose control of our circumstances, God never says, "Oh no, I just turned away for a few seconds." He watches over us—always.

Here's a second amazing truth that can bring us joy even in trials: God is working for His glory and our good in every circumstance of life, the good and the bad. His hand may be hard to trace sometimes, but when you can't see God's hand, you can still trust His heart. "And we know that for those who love God all things work together for good, for those who are called according to his purpose" (Romans 8:28).

This truth also means that God won't abandon His work until it's finished. There is a "way of escape," a back door, for every trial. "No temptation has overtaken you that is not common to man. God is faithful, and he will not let you be tempted beyond your ability, but with the temptation he will also provide the way of escape, that you may be able to endure it" (1 Corinthians 10:13). So when you're in the middle of the griddle, remember that there is a beginning and end as well as a middle to your trial. I love the name that Jesus gives to Himself in Revelation 22:13: "I am the Alpha and the Omega . . . the beginning and the end." Jesus will never leave anything undone in your life.

Warren Wiersbe, a wonderful Bible teacher and author, says that "God has His eye on the clock and His hand on the thermostat" when we go into the furnace of affliction. This is why the Bible can command us, "Give thanks in all circumstances" (1 Thessalonians 5:18). We hear this verse quoted many times, but that's not all it says. Paul continued, "For this is the will of God in Christ Jesus for you." Rejoicing and giving thanks aren't just for the positive thinkers and people who have life going their way. It is God's will that we all thank Him at all times.

WE MUST REJECT THE JOY-KILLERS WHO WANT TO PUT US UNDER BONDAGE

The mood changes between Philippians 3:1 and 3:2 as Paul warns us of those who would steal our joy by destroying our faith. Listen to this implied but clear warning: "Beware of the *joy-killers*! Watch out for the *evildoers*! Run from the *flesh mutilators*! They're out there, and they're coming to your church to devour *you*!"

Look out for the dogs, look out for the evildoers, look out for those who mutilate the flesh. (v. 2)

Who Let the Dogs Out?

These are the Judaizers we mentioned earlier, the legalists who traveled around behind the apostle Paul and distorted the message of the gospel. They were telling believers like those in Philippi that while it was wonderful to accept God's grace and believe in Jesus, they also needed to keep the Law of Moses to be saved—particularly circumcision, which was the outward sign of the old covenant. These people were joy-killers who wanted to put believers back under the bondage of their old way of life.

When Paul called them "dogs," he wasn't referring to household pets that are tame and live the good life. He used a word that referred to the dangerous, mongrel dogs that roamed the streets of cities in the ancient world. I was originally going to call this message, "Who Let the Dogs Out?" because these dogs were out barking and biting and devouring the faith of Christians, trying to steal their joy in Jesus.

Unfortunately, these dogs are still around today. They like to major on the minors and minor on the majors. They may seem harmless, or at least well intentioned, but Paul didn't cut them any slack. He called them "evildoers." They are religious mongrels who will take you from the grace of God to something else.

My friend Franklin Graham caught a lot of flak a few years ago for saying that a religion that promotes terrorism is evil. But I am telling you that any religion based on a works system is evil because it perverts the grace of God found in Christ alone.

The early life of Martin Luther, the great Reformer, is a classic example of sterile, joyless, religious legalism. Luther was trying his best to please God as a monk, working hard to be holy, striving to find the favor and approval of God. He was punishing and tearing his flesh by crawling on his knees up the steps of the church in Rome. But one day he read in the book of Romans, "The righteous shall live by faith" (1:17).

Martin Luther ceased his religious strivings and came to personal faith in Jesus Christ. His life was revolutionized, and he helped change the world.

A new Christian in our church fellowship is another example. This man was a member of a non-Christian religious group, and he told us he was just so tired and exhausted trying to be a good person in his old religion.

That's what religion without Christ will do to you. Religion is joyless and powerless. Forget about religion and follow Jesus.

Joy-Killers Put Their Confidence in the Flesh

Paul had not labored and suffered so hard to bring the Philippians to faith in Christ only to see these false teachers steal them away. While the Judaizers wanted believers to put their confidence in human effort to gain their salvation, Paul said a true believer is one who "put[s] no confidence in the flesh" (Philippians 3:3). He spoke from experience. In Paul's B.C. (before Christ) days, no one had more reason to trust in himself. He owned a remarkable religious pedigree, much better than most, according to verse 4.

This is the reason Paul recited his former status in Judaism (Philippians 3:5–6). The young man known as Saul was "a Hebrew of Hebrews," "of the tribe of Benjamin." He kept the requirements of the Law so strictly that he was "blameless." He was also "a Pharisee"—a term that may have a negative connotation to most people, but not among the Jews. The Pharisees were a spiritually elite group, highly honored and respected as the best of the best.

Paul was a player. A mover and shaker. A spiritual celebrity who would have been listed in the *Time* magazine of ancient Israel as among the top influencers of his day. But Paul was a zealot without grace or mercy. He was also "a persecutor of the church." He was not a joyful believer in God, but an angry, violent man, full of wrath against anyone who didn't follow his religion. Saul of Tarsus was, in short, a religious terrorist.

But when he met Jesus on the Damascus road, Saul the angry persecutor became roadkill. Saul of Tarsus died that day, and when Paul got up off the ground he was a new person in the power of Christ. Saul the murderer became Paul the missionary. That's why he wrote so passionately to the churches about the dangers of false teachers. Paul knew what sterile religion can do to people, and after he met Christ he said his former pedigree and accomplishments were like "rubbish" to him (Philippians 3:8).

Paul lost his reputation, his rank in Judaism, and his man-made righteousness (v. 9), but he gained a relationship with Christ and discovered His resurrection power. Now nothing else mattered. Paul's passion became to "know [Christ] and the power of his resurrection, and [to] share his sufferings, becoming like him in his death, that by any means possible I may attain the resurrection from the dead" (vv. 10–11).

YOU CAN PROTECT YOURSELF AGAINST THE JOY-KILLERS

Paul's biographical account in Philippians 3 is one of the best examples of keeping it real that you will ever read. Paul did a spiritual audit of his life and said in essence, "I had all of this, but adding it all up, it came out to be a loss and not an asset on my spiritual ledger. So I threw it all on the dung heap when I met Christ."

Most people who discover that everything they have ever believed, prepared for, lived for, and accomplished added up to a minus are in despair. But for Paul it became the occasion for overwhelming joy because he met Jesus. If you want to know lasting joy, let me suggest five ways to pursue and develop your relationship with Jesus Christ.

First, get to know Jesus *personally*. The difference between the Christian faith and every other religious system is the person of Jesus Christ who calls us into a vital, personal relationship with Him based on His love and grace alone. Jesus is not Someone to know about, but Someone to know and love.

Second, get to know Christ *powerfully*. Paul wanted to know Christ in the power of His resurrection. Think of it. The power that raised Jesus from the dead is the power available to you and me every day. His powerful presence is living in you!

A third way to know Christ is *passionately*. Now the word *passion* takes on a greater meaning when it is used in connection with Christ's sufferings on the cross. Paul said he wanted to "share his sufferings, becoming like him in his death." Paul was passionate for Christ in the sense of being committed to Him, but he also understood that part of his relationship with Christ was the fellowship of His suffering. For us, this involves offering our lives as a living sacrifice to Him (Romans 12:1). Each day give your life unconditionally to Him, and His joy will fill you.

Number four on this list is to know Christ *progressively*. This refers to our daily growth in Him or sanctification. Are you getting to know Jesus better and better as you walk with Him? The Bible says, "This is the will of God, your sanctification" (1 Thessalonians 4:3).

There is one more way we can know Christ, but it awaits the day when we will see Him face to face. Then we will know Him *perfectly*. Paul said he wanted to do whatever it took to attain the resurrection and be with Christ. Similarly, the psalmist prayed, "As for me, I shall behold your face in righteousness; when I awake, I shall be satisfied with your likeness" (Psalm 17:15).

One of the catchphrases this generation will be remembered for is, *get real*. That's what we're doing as we study the book of Philippians and find out how to be fit for life. There is no great mystery to having joy and peace in your life. It's all found in Jesus Christ.

PART THREE

Going the Distance

CHAPTER ELEVEN

Winning Habits

If art imitates life, maybe we could say that athletics illuminate life. The apostle Paul was familiar with the sports of his day and often used sports metaphors to illustrate spiritual truth. The great apostle enjoyed the athletic arena and the lessons learned there. We see again and again how he compares the Christian life to an athletic contest.

This dynamic leader lived to win and loved to win, not for his own glory, but for the Kingdom of Christ. He was a winning Christian in every good and positive sense of that term. And he challenged every other believer to be a winner because in Christ we can all run a winning race and gain the prize.

This chapter is called "Winning Habits" for a reason. If you want to know how to succeed, then you should study the habits of successful people, whether we're talking about the sports or business world or life in general. With the focus of this book being how to be fit for life, how to make the most of our lives for Christ and His cause, we need to ask ourselves what the most successful and effective Christian who ever lived did in order to maximize his life and influence in the world.

It is always the passion of a winner to excel at the highest level. Any professional athlete will tell you that the worst label to be stuck with is, "This guy has potential." That's the kiss of death because it tells teams that here is a player who hasn't yet arrived and may never live up to that potential. As Christians we are given the most awesome potential possible: "Therefore, if anyone is in Christ, he is a new creation. The old has passed away; behold, the new has come" (2 Corinthians 5:17). It doesn't get any better than that, which is why it is ridiculous for Christians to live bland, anemic lives.

It's time for all followers of Christ to experience the full and abundant life promised by Jesus. Many people want to win but don't have the will to win. Most everybody has a desire to win, but not everybody has the determination to win. Paul had both, and so he was willing to invest in the spiritual training it takes to be a winner for Christ.

I have read that successful Olympic athletes work out an average of four hours a day, 310 days a year, for six years to compete for the gold. Most of us will never be world-class athletes, but God has called us to be world-class Christians who strive for the prize and win it in Christ's name. In Philippians 3:12–14, like an outstanding coach Paul gives us four of his winning habits that we can emulate.

WINNERS IN JESUS CHRIST ARE DISSATISFIED WITH WHERE THEY ARE

The first winning habit that we need to practice is what I call a humble dissatisfaction. I don't mean there has to be something wrong; it's just that we are always to be moving onward and upward. Paul knew he didn't have it made because he said, "Not that I have already obtained this [the prize] or am already perfect, but I press on to make it my own, because Christ Jesus has made me his own. Brothers, I do not consider that I have made it my own"(Philippians 3:12–13a).

We Need to Keep Our Goals Set High

Paul was satisfied with Christ, but he wasn't satisfied with himself. He was content in his salvation, yet he kept moving forward for the prize of Christ's approval and the rewards that come from it. This is what one Bible teacher calls "blessed discontent."

In 1961 Roger Maris of the New York Yankees hit sixty-one home runs to set a new single-season record. A reporter asked Maris the next spring what his goal was for 1962, and Maris said he felt he would be doing well to hit thirty homers. An old player who was long retired scoffed at Maris's statement when he heard it and chastised Maris for setting such low goals for himself. Whatever the pressures were on Roger

Maris to top his feat of 1961, he proved to be a prophet. His home run output for 1962 was thirty-three, barely half his previous total.

I don't know if you're a goal-setter, but Paul was. He wasn't content just to meet the minimum requirements to squeeze into a corner of heaven. Some Christians want to set their lives on cruise control and coast into heaven. But running at an easy pace will get you beaten every time.

There Will Always Be More to Reach for in Christ

Have you discovered that in Christ there's always more? More of His grace to experience, more prayers to be offered, more of God's Word to learn, more to attempt and achieve for the Lord Jesus Christ. Great coaches don't allow players with great ability to settle for mediocrity in performance.

We can't settle for that either. That's why we are to keep our eyes on Jesus instead of on ourselves or on the other runners around us in the race.

Years ago there was a kid in Florida who had the size and strength of an adult by the time he was twelve years old. He was twice the size of other boys, but he still qualified for Little League. He threw so hard as a pitcher that no one could touch him; he had real potential. But he also liked to clown around and didn't really care about learning anything or developing his talent. Baseball was a joke to this kid. Just to annoy his coach, he would deliberately walk the bases loaded and then strike out the side, laughing as the coach sputtered at him in total frustration.

That kind of clowning, halfhearted effort doesn't have any place in the Christian life. The great thing about our race is that we don't all have to be the biggest or the fastest. We just have to run our race, and we'll receive the prize from Christ. There will always be a tension to the Christian life between dissatisfaction with our current spiritual condition and the desire to move ahead as we strain for the prize.

WINNERS IN JESUS CHRIST HAVE A HEARTFELT CONCENTRATION

A second winning habit Paul revealed in Philippians 3 is a heartfelt concentration. That focus is seen in the words, "One thing I do" (v. 13). We discussed this at some length in a previous chapter, so I'll just remind you that the emphasis in the original language is on the word "one." The idea is that Paul did this one single, solitary thing and let go of anything else that might distract him.

We Need to Keep Our Goals Set High

The question you might have is, what is that one thing? The answer is very simple really. Ask yourself, what is my passion? What do I love to do? Martin Luther said, "If you want to know the will of God, love God with all your heart, mind, soul, and strength, and then do what you want." The psalmist said, "Delight yourself in the LORD, and he will give you the desires of your heart" (Psalm 37:4). The details will differ for each of us, but the basic answer is the same: our abiding passion is the pursuit of Christ and our relationship with Him.

Pat Williams, the executive vice-president of the Orlando Magic basketball team, is the author of thirty-six books and a well-known speaker. He was once asked what constituted success. Pat, a committed Christian, answered, "Figure out what you love doing as young as possible, and organize your life around determining how to make a living at it."

That's good advice. I can't tell you what that "one thing" is for you, but I know what it will take for you to achieve it. Here's an example of what not to do. Some years ago there was a football player who had the potential (there's that word again) to be an outstanding lineman. But as much as this guy wanted to play pro football, he apparently liked food even more. He was an undisciplined eater who gained so much weight that he literally ate himself out of his career.

Someone who watched this happen observed wryly, "There were only two things standing between him and true greatness: a knife and a fork!"

This man allowed himself to become distracted from the goal. A successful athlete is one who is able to practice discipline in order to achieve success.

When I was a small child, my grandfather took me down to the Western Auto store in our little Arkansas town before Easter and bought some cute little chicks whose feathers had been dyed the various colors of Easter eggs. I loved those little chicks, but it wasn't too long before the colors wore off as they grew, and we wound up with four or five big white chickens running around in the yard. That wasn't good, according to my grandfather, who saw in them several good meals.

My grandfather also decided for some reason that I needed to witness the execution. So despite my tears he took a couple of the chickens to the backyard, where he twisted the heads off of those chickens. Of course, their bodies didn't know they were dead, so they ran around frantically in all directions until the twitching in their muscles stopped. Naturally, I was horrified. But today I know that too many believers are roaming around like chickens with their heads off!

There are a lot of good things you can do, but only one best thing, and achieving that best thing requires focus and discipline. When I played college baseball, we weren't much different than other university athletes. We wanted to get practice over with so we could eat, see our girlfriends, relax, or do homework—usually in that order.

But the coach wouldn't let us go until we had run through the same drills and plays so many times, we could do them without even having to think about it. That was the point, of course, because during the game you often don't have time to think about what you need to do. You just have time to act and react.

We Need to Discard the Distractions to Keep Our Concentration

The writer of Hebrews also used a sports reference when he said, "Therefore, since we are surrounded by so great a cloud of witnesses, let us also lay aside every weight, and sin which clings so closely, and let us run with endurance the race that is set before us" (12:1). Sin is what drags us down and keeps us from winning the race. It's like trying to run with heavy weights tied around our ankles.

But there are other things that may not be blatant sin but still serve to distract us. Some Christians don't have time for spiritual development because they are either too busy doing other things or are undisciplined in their habits and spend too much time just hanging out.

A winning attitude demands intense concentration. Successful Christians, like successful athletes, give up a lot of other things to focus on the one thing they know God wants them to do. There are many things we can do, but there's really only one thing that's important, and that's the prize.

And by the way, you only have to worry about your own "one thing." In the Christian race, no one has to lose; so you and I can both win. We're not in competition with other Christians, and we don't run to impress others. So you can run your own race without having to keep looking around to see how everyone else is doing. Stay in your own lane, do what God has called you to do, and your prize will be waiting for you at the finish line when Jesus says, "Well done, good and faithful servant."

WINNERS IN JESUS CHRIST DISPLAY A HOLY DETERMINATION

Winning habit number three is the corollary of number two: a holy determination. Paul wrote, "Forgetting what lies behind and straining forward to what lies ahead, I press on toward the goal for the prize of the upward call of God in Christ Jesus" (Philippians 3:13–14). The phrase I want you to see is "press on," which literally means "to stretch." It's the picture of a runner straining forward with every muscle and every ounce of energy to break the tape and win the race.

It takes that kind of determined attitude to win in the Christian life. American Christianity is all caught up in prosperity and ease and comfort. We know very little of sacrifice and determination to press on against all odds. Being determined to win doesn't mean we never fail or get knocked down. But the winners are those who get up and keep on playing through the disappointment and pain.

I'm sure somebody must have said to Paul at some point, "Why don't you just quit? You've been beaten, you're chained in prison, and you must be worn out. Why don't you just cut your losses and call it a day?" But Paul's answer would have been, "It's too early to quit. I can keep going because Christ strengthens me. I'll keep pressing on as long as He gives me breath."

That's the holy determination it takes to finish the race and win the prize. Many of us are good starters but poor finishers. Paul's determination to finish well paid off because he was able to say at the end of his life, "I have fought the good fight, I have finished the race, I have kept the faith" (2 Timothy 4:7).

But before you think that winning is only for spiritual giants like Paul, go on to verse 8: "Henceforth there is laid up for me the crown of righteousness, which the Lord, the righteous judge, will award to me on that Day, and not only to me but also to all who have loved his appearing." Strive for the prize!

WINNERS IN JESUS CHRIST HAVE A HEAVENLY MOTIVATION

We're almost done with this workout session in our effort to become fit for life. A fourth winning habit in Philippians 3 is a heavenly motivation, or what Paul referred to as "the upward call" in verse 14.

Heavenly Motivation Requires a Forward Focus

There's only one direction for the Christian, and that is onward and upward. Our Lord and our prize await us at the end of the race. Part of heeding the upward call is "forgetting what lies behind" (v. 13). Satchel Paige, the legendary baseball pitcher and dugout philosopher, used to say, "Don't look back. Something may be gaining on you."

As Christians our motivation should not just be to outrun the past with its mistakes and failures. And on the other hand, if we are forgiven, why would we want to live in the past? Neither should we hang on to past successes if they're keeping us from moving onward and upward. Someone has said that successes are harder for most people to get over than failures.

One place where we often see the truth of this is with retired athletes who were stars in their days. One of the hardest things for them to do is put away the old press clippings from their playing days and move on. A lot of old ballplayers live in the past.

Unfortunately, many Christians do the same. I've been in church all my life, and I've heard many testimonies about what God did thirty years ago. My question is, what is God doing in your life today? Are you living for Christ today? Please get past the past. You can't go forward looking in the rearview mirror.

Don't Let the Obstacles Trip You Up

Paul said he was focused on the upward call. That didn't mean his journey was a straight line with no detours or distractions. But he didn't let the obstacles become the object of his passion or obsession. The hurdles in a race are there to challenge the runners to soar high, not to trip them or cause them to turn back.

So run hard—and don't forget to enjoy the race along the way. Putting in the time and commitment necessary to win the prize from Christ and the approval of Christ is meant to be a joyful experience. I want to have the spirit of Eric Liddell, the great Olympic star and missionary to China whose life was profiled in the movie *Chariots of Fire*. Liddell told his sister, "God made me fast, and when I run I feel His pleasure."

I pray that you will feel God's pleasure as you apply Paul's winning habits to your life. Not everybody can be a winner on the court or track or field, but every Christian can be a winner in the race for God's prize.

CHAPTER TWELVE

The Ultimate Extreme Makeover

Perhaps you have heard the story of the old farmer who takes his family to town for the first time. His wife wants to go see the stores, so the farmer and his son wander the streets, mesmerized by the sights and sounds of the city.

On one street the farmer and his son come upon a bank. The farmer peers in the window just in time to see a feeble, white-haired woman being escorted through a giant metal door. Not knowing what a vault is, the farmer stares intently at the door to see what is going to happen. A few minutes later, a very attractive young woman walks out.

The farmer draws in his breath, rubs his eyes, and looks again. Sure enough, the young woman is still there. That's enough for the old man. He turns to his son and says in a solemn tone, "Boy, go get your mother!"

A lot of people wish it would be this easy to get the extreme make-over they want so badly. A bank vault won't do the job—although it wouldn't hurt to own one if you're planning to get all your parts lifted, nipped, tucked, or otherwise enhanced. But the fact is that if you are a child of God, you *will* have an extreme makeover someday, and it will happen faster than you could walk in and out of a bank vault.

The Bible says, "We shall all be changed, in a moment, in the twinkling of an eye, at the last trumpet. For the trumpet will sound, and the dead will be raised imperishable, and we shall be changed"

(1 Corinthians 15:51–52). At the Second Coming of Jesus Christ, we will experience the ultimate extreme makeover when we receive our resurrection bodies. Actually, the believer's makeover starts at salvation, as Paul wrote: "If anyone is in Christ, he is a new creation. The old has passed away; behold, the new has come" (2 Corinthians 5:17). But instead of starting on the outside, as the world does, our makeover begins on the inside, in our spirits, and someday will be visible to everyone on the outside in our new bodies.

What I'm talking about are the three tenses of salvation. We *have been saved*. That happened the moment we put our faith in Christ and were forgiven of our sins. This is the past tense of salvation—but don't let that term throw you because salvation is a past action that has ongoing results. The Bible calls this our *justification*, a legal term that means to be declared righteous. This happens as our spirits are instantly and forever regenerated or made alive in Christ. You will never be more justified than you were the day you cried out to Jesus to save you from your sins.

We are also *being saved*, which is the present tense of salvation. This involves the process we have discussed at several points along the way—our sanctification or progressive growth in the grace of Christ. Since we are three-part beings—body, soul, and spirit—we can equate sanctification with our soul or psyche, the part of us that includes our intellect and emotions by which we interact with life around us.

In sanctification we are being made more like Jesus Christ as His righteousness is applied in our lives. This part of our spiritual makeover is a work in progress, and some believers are definitely more attractive than others when it comes to displaying a Christlike attitude of love and self-denial. It is also a lifelong process, so none of us has to worry about becoming *too* beautiful. When boxer Muhammad Ali was still a brash, young Cassius Clay, he used to crow, "I'm too pretty." Not to worry; we'll never be able to say that.

Salvation also has a future tense because one day, when Christ comes for us, we will be *fully and finally saved*. This is our glorification, of which Paul wrote in 1 Corinthians 15 and elsewhere. This aspect of salvation relates to our bodies, when our makeover is complete.

So we can summarize the process of our extreme spiritual makeover this way: We are justified immediately in our spirits, we are saved or sanctified progressively in our souls, and we will be saved ultimately when our bodies are glorified. One day people are going to look at you in your new, perfect, glorified body and say, "You look marvelous!" And it won't cost you a bank vault's worth of money to get it.

Our salvation is signed and sealed; so we don't have to keep running back to the altar every week or month to get "resaved." Our glorification awaits the day of God's choosing, so we can only look forward to it. But in between there is a lot we can do to cooperate with the Holy Spirit as He makes us over into the image of Christ. Our goal should be to look as beautiful for Jesus, if I can use that word, as it is possible for us to be this side of heaven. This process is what Philippians 3:17–21 is all about.

TO BE MADE OVER WE MUST FOLLOW GODLY EXAMPLES

One way we can experience a makeover from the inside out is to follow godly examples. Paul wrote, "Brothers, join in imitating me, and keep your eyes on those who walk according to the example you have in us" (Philippians 3:17).

Paul was not afraid to say, "Imitate me." To the Corinthians he wrote, "Be imitators of me, as I am of Christ" (1 Corinthians 11:1). That last phrase is the key. Paul wasn't being arrogant. He had already told the Philippians that he hadn't yet arrived (3:12). But he knew that Christians need a godly example to follow. His change to the plural "us" in verse 17 was likely a reference to Timothy and Epaphroditus, whose worthy examples he had already mentioned, and perhaps others in Philippi who were worth imitating.

Be Careful Who You Choose as Your Heroes and Examples

You can tell a lot about a person by his or her heroes. A short time before the terrible massacre at Virginia Tech, a teenager in Texas shocked everyone by going next door and shooting another teen, seriously wounding him. The shooter had given no outward indication of being a troubled person and was eventually released on bail to his parents.

But just as the nation was reeling from the Virginia Tech episode, investigators on the case here in Texas discovered that the teen who shot his neighbor had expressed admiration for serial killers and said he wanted to be like them. His bail was quickly revoked, and he was jailed to await trial.

That's an extreme example, but we do tend to become like the people we admire. That's why the Bible tells us not to follow fools: "Bad company ruins good morals" (1 Corinthians 15:33), and "The companion of fools will suffer harm" (Proverbs 13:20).

If you are a baby boomer you may have received one of those "then and now" e-mails from a friend, the ones that compare us in the sixties to today. One of these comparisons says: "In the sixties, trying desperately to look like Elizabeth Taylor and Marlon Brando. Today, trying desperately *not* to look like Elizabeth Taylor and Marlon Brando."

That's pretty well the way it goes, isn't it? But while a person's human heroes may age and fade, if we are following people who are following Christ, that inner beauty doesn't have to fade but can grow more attractive every day. It reminds me of a book written by football player Joe Namath, another sports figure from the sixties who, like Muhammad Ali, liked to admire himself. Namath's book was modestly titled *I Can't Wait Until Tomorrow . . . 'Cause I Get Better-Looking Every Day.*

All of Us Need People to Be Our Models, Mentors, and Motivators

Well, in the spiritual sense being models for others can and should be our goal as we reflect the grace and beauty of Christ. Paul could say with true humility, "If you want to know what the Christian life looks like, look at me." If we want to go forward in our Christian lives, we need to associate with people who are living the life and are out ahead of us. That person could be a parent, a pastor or other spiritual leader, or a friend. But choose well the people you choose to follow.

Every person needs a model, a mentor, and a motivator. These could all be the same person, but usually we need several good and godly examples to follow. What I'm talking about is different than putting your faith in another person. We don't look to people for our faith, but to Jesus alone. If we put too much stock in people, we could be disappointed because people fail. But that doesn't absolve us of our responsibility to choose good examples and to be good examples ourselves.

To Be Made Over We Must Flee from Dangerous Enemies

Unfortunately, godly examples aren't the only kind out there. Paul had to deal with the enemies of the faith because these people were all around: "For many, of whom I have often told you and now tell you even with tears, walk as enemies of the cross of Christ. Their end is destruction, their god is their belly, and they glory in their shame, with minds set on earthly things" (Philippians 3:18–19).

If we follow after these kinds of individuals we will not only fall but will collapse beyond the point of recovery. That's why we need to be forewarned so we can be forearmed against the enemies of Christ who assault and attack us in order to lead us astray from following hard after Him.

Watch Out for People Who Worship Their Sensual Appetites

Paul said of these people that, if I can paraphrase, their deity is their belly. They worship their sensual appetites and desires. These are people who live by the ancient philosophy that Paul referred to in 1 Corinthians 15: "Let us eat and drink, for tomorrow we die" (v. 32). Look back just a few paragraphs in this chapter and you'll recall that verse 33 of this same chapter of 1 Corinthians warns against corrupting ourselves with bad companions. The reason they're bad is because they worship pleasure instead of worshiping God.

God's house is not an animal house. An animal only lives for three things—self-preservation, self-propagation, and self-gratification. That's how a lot of people live, even some who claim to be followers of Jesus Christ. Their mouths may speak of heaven, but their minds and hearts are set on the things of the world.

The problem with this kind of life is that the road to pleasure is a dead-end. While sin may briefly gratify, it can never satisfy. It's true that sin brings pleasure for a season. The Bible acknowledges "the fleeting pleasures of sin" (Hebrews 11:25). We make a mistake if we tell people there is no pleasure in sin. But when that short season is over, there's hell to pay because Paul said the end of people who live by their sensual appetites is destruction, an eternity of torturous pain separated from the presence of God forever. That would be hell.

We sometimes hear people saying foolish things like, "Well, I'd rather be with my friends and buddies in hell. We're going to have a great time down there." But there are no parties in hell, no fun and games in a Christless eternity. Isolation and separation await those who reject God. The rich man in hell whom Jesus talked about in Luke 16:19–31 begged for just a drop of water to cool his tongue. Imagine thirsting forever and never being satisfied.

Paul also said the enemies of the cross "glory in their shame." This could be the motto of our generation. Shameful lifestyles and affairs that we never dreamed would even be publicized are glamorized and glorified. Enemies of the cross are people "who call evil good and good evil" (Isaiah 5:20). God says that a day is coming when this parading of the flesh, this shamefulness of people who consider their shame their glory and their perversion their popularity, will all be over. Our responsibility is to avoid mimicking their example.

Our Task Is to Reach out to These Enemies with the Love of Christ

But Paul was certainly not advocating hatred of the ungodly. He wrote to the Philippians through his tears as he thought of lost souls destined for an eternal hell. Paul wept over these enemies of the cross because Jesus died for them too. It's good to remind ourselves regularly that it is not God's desire "that any should perish, but that all should reach repentance" (2 Peter 3:9).

If we want to be like Christ, we will love the people He loves. And while we don't want to imitate them, it ought to be our constant concern and burden to bring the lost to Jesus Christ. They need someone to point them in the right direction, and that someone is you and me.

TO BE MADE OVER WE MUST FOCUS ON A BEAUTIFUL ETERNITY

If you want to experience God's extreme makeover, you also need to keep your eyes on the goal of an eternity with Christ in the glories of heaven. That's why Paul said, "But our citizenship is in heaven, and from it we await a Savior, the Lord Jesus Christ, who will transform our lowly body to be like his glorious body, by the power that enables him even to subject all things to himself" (Philippians 3:20–21).

We are citizens of another kingdom, an eternal one. Our citizenship papers have already been transferred to heaven. Our names are written down there, our future is there, our hope is there, and our Savior is there! So we don't want to live as if this life is all there is or as if the here-and-now is all we have to look forward to.

We Have a Glorious Future Awaiting Us in Heaven

Let me tell you, if your hope is fixed on this earth, you will be disappointed. The famous physicist Stephen Hawking said recently that he believes mankind's only hope for survival is in outer space because he sees no future for us on earth. One of the original seven U.S. astronauts, Walter "Wally" Schirra, who died recently, had a discouraging word along that line. He was quoted as saying something along these lines: "Please take care of Mother Earth because I've been out there and I didn't see anyplace else to go."

How refreshing to turn from the pessimism of this age and focus our eyes on heaven, longing for the day when Jesus will be revealed. We must live as heaven-hearted people with our minds on eternal things as we eagerly await Jesus Christ.

That is hope and certainty, not wishful thinking. Heaven is a sure thing for those who know Jesus. We have an eye on the sky, and we're motivated by the fact that Christ is coming again. The Bible even gives us several traits that will help tell us if we are truly living with the return of Christ and heaven's values in view.

People Who Live for Heaven Have a Different Focus on Earth

The first trait is that we will have an intense urgency about our witness for Christ because we know He is coming. Paul said of his ministry, "Necessity is laid upon me. Woe to me if I do not preach the gospel!" (1 Corinthians 9:16), and "Knowing the fear of the Lord, we persuade others" (2 Corinthians 5:11). That's true urgency. I wouldn't want my worst enemy, let alone my best friend, to be lost without Christ forever.

A second trait or quality of people who are looking for Jesus is an intense desire to live the holy life that He desires us to live. The Scripture says, "We know that when he [Jesus] appears we shall be like him, because we shall see him as he is. And everyone who thus hopes in him purifies himself as he is pure" (1 John 3:2–3).

What keeps us motivated to live a godly life is knowing that Christ will come and that we are accountable to Him for our lives. Earlier the apostle John wrote, "Little children, abide in him, so that when he appears we may have confidence and not shrink from him in shame at his coming" (1 John 2:28).

At Christ's coming our spiritual and even bodily makeover will finally be complete. When Jesus comes for us, our bodies will be redeemed from the corruption of this earth. They will be perfect bodies because they will be like Jesus' body after His resurrection.

Right now our bodies are decaying and dying—and some of us look a little further along than others! There's nothing wrong with trying to get and stay fit and preserve life in its fullness. Good physical fitness on the part of Christians who want to honor God's temple is one of the themes of this book. But while we can slow the approach of death, we cannot prevent it. Nor should we want to because it is in the absence from these bodies that we are present with the Lord (2 Corinthians 5:8).

Every day until then we want to get stronger and stronger, but ultimately we will be in that perfected state in which we will serve Christ full-out forever and never grow tired. We will serve Christ in the power of His resurrection because sin will no longer drag us down. We will have been liberated from all of that.

Whenever I think of heaven, some very special people come to mind. My father was murdered during a robbery in his hardware store in Fort Worth in the summer of 1970, just after my wife Deb and I got married, while we were college students. And within eighteen months of that tragedy, Deb's father, Doyle Peters, died of cancer in his early forties.

Doyle Peters was known as Poss around Mineral Wells, Texas. Poss became a believer in Christ as a young man, and he really began living for Christ and became very active in his church. He was very bright, a graduate of Texas Tech with a math degree. He taught and tutored math all of his life. He was so committed to his faith and loved to share Christ. He worked in the bus ministry of the First Baptist Church of Mineral Wells and taught a boys' Sunday school class. Mr. Peters was much beloved in that community.

One day he noticed a lump under his arm. The doctors checked it out, and the diagnosis of advanced melanoma cancer came back. We did everything we could for him, but before we knew it, he was in a coma and near death.

Deb and I came in one weekend from college to visit her father, but he was not communicative. However, as we were sitting there quietly just thinking and praying, Poss began to talk. As we listened, we realized that in his mind he was teaching his Sunday school class. He was telling his boys about Jesus, and then he said, "Okay boys, before we go, let's sing 'When the Roll Is Called Up Yonder.'" Poss began to sing, and I'll never forget hearing:

When the trumpet of the Lord shall sound
And time shall be no more
When the morning breaks eternal, bright and fair–
When the saved of earth shall gather
Over on the other shore
And the roll is called up yonder, I'll be there!

Deb and I joined in singing with him, and a few days later he was gone. But because the name of Doyle Peters was written on the roll of heaven, he is there today—no longer in a body riddled by cancer, but perfect like Christ. The psalmist said, "As for me, I shall behold your face in righteousness; when I awake, I shall be satisfied with your likeness" (Psalm 17:15). There can be no greater goal for our ultimate extreme makeover than to be fully and completely in the likeness of Jesus Christ.

CHAPTER THIRTEEN

Contented Christians

The anthem of my generation back in the 1960s was the song "(I Can't Get No) Satisfaction" by the Rolling Stones. This song was the first smash #1 hit for the Stones in America, and lead singer Mick Jagger, who helped write it, said it transformed the band from just another group into a big-time band.

I don't know if Mick Jagger and the Stones ever found the satisfaction they were looking for, even though they tried and they tried and they tried. Somehow I doubt it—at least not the kind of satisfaction that lasts. That's because lasting satisfaction or contentment is found only in a right relationship with God through Jesus Christ. This alone can give us inner peace that will help make us fit for life.

My good friend Dr. Neil Clark Warren, a well-known Christian psychologist and founder of the eharmony.com web site that matches singles, said, "The secret of contentment lies in discovering who in the world you are and mobilizing your courage to be that person."

That's a great definition of contentment. When you discover who you are in Christ and then have the courage to be the person God has called and equipped you to be, you will be on the road to abiding peace and satisfaction. In short, you will be a contented Christian.

That's worth a lot, because I don't know if you have noticed, but it's hard to find people who are truly content with the way God has made them and what He has given them. They're like Bigfoot—something everybody has heard about and a lot of people believe exists, but something that's hard to verify because sightings are rare.

I heard about a worker in an office who didn't know the boss was standing nearby. This guy said to a coworker, "If I just had a thousand dollars, I'd be really content."

Hearing that, the boss immediately stepped forward, pulled out his checkbook, and started writing. The startled worker asked him what he was doing. "I'm writing you a check for a thousand dollars," the boss replied.

"Why are you doing that?"

"Because I've never met a truly contented person, and I just want to see what one looks like." Sure enough, as soon as the boss had left, the man said to his friend, "I wish I'd asked for two thousand."

Whether that boss had spent one or two thousand dollars, there's a much less expensive way to satisfy that need. The Bible gives us a picture of what a contented Christian would look like. I want to consider four elements that make up the portrait of a believer who can say as Paul said, "I have learned in whatever situation I am to be content" (Philippians 4:11).

A CONTENTED CHRISTIAN IS ONE WHO KNOWS HOW TO PRAY CONFIDENTLY

We will discuss Philippians 4:6 in the next chapter, but I want to piggyback on that study and broaden the principle of prayer to all believers as we consider what it takes to be contented Christians. This great verse says, "Do not be anxious about anything, but in everything by prayer and supplication with thanksgiving let your requests be made known to God."

Prayer Is to Be the Pattern and Practice of Our Lives

It's hard to miss the emphasis that we are to pray about "everything." Paul put it this way in Ephesians 6:18: "praying at all times in the Spirit, with all prayer and supplication." Prayer is not just a flare we send up to God in an emergency, like the soldier who prayed in the foxhole, "God, if You will just get me out of this one, I'll never bother You again."

That's not prayer because prayer is to be the pattern and the practice of a believer's life. In fact, we could say that prayer *is* bothering God, in the sense that we are encouraged to come to Him continually with our needs (though He is not bothered by our coming—He delights to hear from His people). It also involves our worship and adoration of God, expressed in the meaning of the word that Paul used for "prayer" in Philippians 4:6. It carries the idea of being in a kneeling or prone position.

This same word is used in Luke 22:45 when it says that Jesus "rose from prayer" when He had finished praying in the Garden of Gethsemane. The Scripture says that Jesus "fell on the ground" (Mark 14:35) to pray, a picture of complete humility and submission to God. When we practice God's presence every day by coming before Him in humble, adoring prayer, it's pretty hard to live with deep anxiety, discontent, and worry at the same time. Of course, we can pray in any position, but when we pray we bow our hearts to Him.

Worry Is the Enemy of Contentment

Worry is not only the antithesis of prayerful trust, but it is in reality an insult to God's promise of His abiding peace. The picture of this "peace" in Philippians 4:7 is that of a soldier who walks sentry duty around the top of a castle or a fort, guarding against the approach of the enemy.

I don't know of too many enemies that will attack us with more firepower than worry. Too many of us are anxiety addicts. We worry about everything. You've probably heard that 90 percent of the things we worry about never happen, and the other 10 percent are mostly things we couldn't change anyway.

Worry is wasteful because it dissipates your strength, destroys your spirit, and robs you of the contentment God has promised to those who rest and trust in Him. Worry will wreak havoc upon you physically and emotionally as well as spiritually. Dr. Charles Mayo, the founder of the famed Mayo Clinic, spoke about the physical effects of worry when he said, "I have never known a man to die of overwork, but many who died of worry."

Worry also chokes us emotionally. Did you know that the Anglo-Saxon word for *worry* described a wolf strangling a little lamb? Worry is emotional strangulation that will cut you off from the breath and the power of God in your life. We tend to make light of our tendency to worry with statements like, "Well, that's just the way God made me." No, it isn't, or the Bible would not command us not to worry. Worry is a lack of faith, not a personality trait. Worry begins where faith ends. Someone said, "Worry slanders every promise in the Word of God."

Worry is a major spiritual problem in too many Christians' lives, and the result is no contentment or peace. The old Sunday school chorus asked, "Why worry when you can pray?" If we were honest, a lot of us would have to change that to, "Why pray when you can worry?" The Bible tells us not to worry about anything because there is no problem too big for God to solve. But it is also true that there is no problem too *small* for God to solve. Can you think of any problem in your life that's not small to God?

God Urges Us to Pray about Everything

Paul also used the word "supplication" in Philippians 4:6 in conjunction with our requests. Not only are we to pray about our worries and give them to God, but we can also pray about our desires. Prayer is not an attempt to convince a reluctant God to open His hand and share a few blessings with us. He loves to give us the desires of our hearts when we are in right relationship with Him. "Delight yourself in the LORD, and he will give you the desires of your heart" (Psalm 37:4).

If you want to be contented in your life, pray constantly and confidently—asking, seeking, and knocking instead of worrying and fretting.

A CONTENTED CHRISTIAN IS ONE WHO KNOWS HOW TO THINK DIFFERENTLY

The book of Philippians is filled with great verses to memorize. Here's one that ought to be in your memory bank: "Whatever is true, whatever is honorable, whatever is just, whatever is pure, whatever is lovely, whatever is commendable, if there is any excellence, if there is anything worthy of praise, think about these things" (4:8).

Our minds are constantly being bombarded by negative, defiling, destructive thoughts. So if we are going to find contentment we need to eliminate these evil thoughts and concentrate on what is good, wholesome, and holy.

You may say, "That's hard to do." Of course, it's hard to do. If it were easy, everybody could do it. But remember that the Christian's motto is, "I can do all things through him who strengthens me" (Philippians 4:13).

The reason we can control our thoughts through the power of Christ is that God has so designed us that we can only think one thought at a time. So I can't be thinking the right things and the wrong things at the same time. That's why it is so important for us to fill our minds with good and godly things. Proverbs 4:23 says, "Keep your heart with all vigilance, for from it flow the springs of life."

This verse teaches that the thoughts and imaginations we allow to develop in our minds have a dramatic effect on the choices we make in life. The longer I live, the more I believe that the way we think and the attitude in which we think is the most important part of our lives because our thoughts produce our actions, our actions produce our habits, and our habits produce our character.

God's Word Will Completely Transform Our Minds

If we are going to be successful and prosperous and blessed, we must sit at the feet of Jesus and His Word. When I talk about changing our thoughts, I'm not talking about behavior modification or self-talk but rather meditating and concentrating upon the Word of God. The more and more we get the Word of God in us, the more we will be transformed by the renewing of our minds. As we read in Romans 12:2, "Do not be conformed to this world, but be transformed by the renewal of your mind, that by testing you may discern what is the will of God, what is good and acceptable and perfect." It is the power of God's Word as we meditate upon it that keeps us from failure and sinful behavior. Scripture says, "How can a young man keep his way pure? By guarding it according to your word" (Psalm 119:9), and "Your word is a lamp to my feet and a light to my path" (Psalm 119:105).

When you live the Word of God, your life will be transformed by its truth. A contented Christian is one who thinks differently than the world thinks and therefore lives differently than the world lives.

A CONTENTED CHRISTIAN IS ONE WHO KNOWS HOW TO LIVE GRATEFULLY

Philippians 4:6 also urges the Christian to pray "with thanksgiving" in your heart. Gratitude and contentment are two sides of the same coin. Grateful people are joyous people because they understand that life is a gift from God. Gratitude recognizes that we are dependent upon God, which is why Scripture says, "There is great gain in godliness with contentment" (1 Timothy 6:6).

Gratitude Knows When to Say Enough Is Enough

We all want to achieve things in life, and we live in a part of the world where achievement is possible beyond most people's wildest dreams. God made us to be creative and to seek to use the gifts He has given us, but there also has to come a point at which we say enough is enough.

Many Americans have never really stopped to ask themselves, "How much money do I have to make to be happy?" and come up with a satisfying answer. They just know it isn't the amount they're making now. The same can be said of things such as their home. They don't know how big a home it will take to make them feel content. They just know they can't be fully content in the house they have.

What is it going to take for us to be content and satisfied in life? The truly rich are those who have learned to live with the things that money can't buy, and even to live without many things that money can buy. I encourage you to sit down someday and make a list of the things you would be content to live without. You might find that list is a lot longer than you would think at first.

Finding Real Contentment Is a Lifelong Learning Process

Paul's statement in Philippians 4:11 is a model for us: "I have *learned* in whatever situation I am to be content" (emphasis added). He was saying that this didn't come to him naturally. He actually borrowed a word from the mystery religions of the ancient world, a word that meant to learn the supposed divine secrets that would make them fulfilled and happy. (And you thought the best-selling New Age book *The Secret* was something new!) The Word of God gives us the real secret to life—contentment.

Sometimes we get the idea that Paul was a martyr at heart who kind of enjoyed being beaten, hungry, thirsty, cold, shipwrecked, destitute, and facing all of the other hardships he endured.

Not at all. Paul wasn't any different than the rest of us in that he liked to eat and have a warm place to sleep. But he loved Jesus more than he loved the comforts of life, and so he learned the lesson of contentment whether he had food or not. Contentment is a lifelong learning process, and most of us have a long way to go.

There's a lot of talk these days about simplifying life and living on less. I'm not suggesting you have to sell everything and live on bread and water—although some people probably need an extreme wake-up call like that in terms of their consumption and consumerism. The contentment the Scripture speaks of is an attitude of the heart that says, "Thank You, Lord" whether the meal is a steak or a salad. A wonderful old hymn says, "What He takes or what He gives us, shows the Father's love so precious." When you can sing that from your heart, you're on the pathway to becoming a contented Christian.

A CONTENTED CHRISTIAN IS ONE WHO KNOWS HOW TO STAND BOLDLY

Paul wanted the believers in Philippi to be able to stand boldly for Christ, both in terms of godly living and standing against the enemies of the faith and the perversion of the gospel. Under the inspiration of the Holy Spirit, the apostle was able to say, "What you have learned and received and heard and seen in me—practice these things, and the God of peace will be with you" (Philippians 4:9). This last phrase reminds us that true contentment can be found in living full-throttle for Jesus, with nothing held back.

I want to be able to stand boldly for Christ, both as a pastor who is leading a church and as a Christian who wants his life to count for Christ. There are some disciplines I practice each day that help me be a bold believer. I want to share these with you.

Give All of Your Desires and Expectations to Christ

We could say that a Christian is a person who has no expectations except those God gives. We are like soldiers awaiting the instructions of our commanding officer. Now there's nothing wrong with having desires and dreams for your life. Just make sure that you don't become so fixated on them that they become the "god" of your life, something you just have to do or be in order to be content.

The best way to ensure that the plans you have don't begin to have you is to give them to God on a daily basis. That's part of what it means to offer yourself to God as "a living sacrifice" (Romans 12:1). Before your feet hit the floor, say, "Lord Jesus, today my life is Yours." Ask the Spirit of God to fill you. Give all earthly things to Christ so you can focus on eternal things. You will never stand stronger than when you are standing firm in the power of Christ, fully yielded to Him.

Realize That Every Day and Everything Is a Gift from God

Anything and everything that enters our lives as children of God comes from the Father's hand and is filtered through His loving heart. If I know that my Father in heaven loves me with perfect love, I can stand in bold assurance against anything that comes my way. We don't have to live wringing our hands and worrying about what's going to happen to us tomorrow. We don't have to be addicted to our anxieties when we understand that we are in the providential plan and care of God. I've said several times that whatever happens to me as God's child is for my good and His glory—and that's an unbeatable combination.

See Every Life Experience as an Opportunity to Praise God

Most people's thoughts don't turn to worship after they have suffered a defeat of some sort. But a truly contented Christian can say even in heartache or discouragement, "Lord, You are my strength and my portion, my song and my joy."

There is a very poignant example of this in 2 Samuel 12, which is part of the aftermath of the infamous story of King David's sin with Bathsheba. Even though the baby who was born from that union was conceived in sin, David prayed fervently that his little son might live. David spent days on his face, pleading with God without eating or doing anything else.

But after the baby died, the Scripture says, "David arose from the earth and washed and anointed himself and changed his clothes. And he went into the house of the LORD and worshiped" (2 Samuel 12:20). David's sin had been exposed, and he had repented and had been graciously forgiven by God. But David also understood that God deserved his worship even when the answer to his prayer was no. There was a sense of closure and even a peacefulness about what David did, which brings me to the final thing I try to do each day to be a strong, contented Christian.

Rest in God's Wisdom and Trust His Goodness

Any soldier who knows how to stand at attention properly will tell you that you won't stand for very long if you lock your knees and go rigid. The blood supply will be cut off, and you'll faint. The trick is to stand erect but relax your knees in their natural position.

Much the same is true in the Christian life. Standing boldly for Christ doesn't demand a rigid stance that slowly cuts off your blood supply. We can rest in the Lord's care and relax in His arms even as we stand for Him. And this, by the way, is also a formula for real contentment.

I begin my day with a prayer that includes something like this: "Lord, I know that even in the tough times You are building and strengthening my character, and therefore today I rest and trust in You, knowing that You want what is best for me." My prayer for you is that you will experience the kind of godly contentment and holy boldness that make a difference for Christ.

CHAPTER FOURTEEN

Live to Give

One of the best stories of selfless giving I've found in a long time is the "secret Santa" who has become a local legend in the Kansas City area.

This red-shirted giver passes out $100 bills to random people during the holidays—and this has been going on for over twenty years. A few years ago, he gave out a total of $40,000!

The story behind this is as intriguing as the man's identity, which was revealed in 2006 when he was diagnosed with cancer. Kansas City's "Secret Santa" was a millionaire businessman named Larry Stewart, who has since died of his disease. The saga began in 1971 when he was an out-of-work salesman living in his car in the town of Houston, Mississippi. The kindly owner of a diner gave him $20 for breakfast and a tank of gas to drive out of town.

Eight years later this formerly broke salesman was a successful businessman. One day just before Christmas he gave a carhop at a drive-in a $20 tip, and her eyes filled with tears as she told him he had no idea how much his gift meant. The man recalled the diner owner's kindness and said, "A lightbulb went off in my head that now was the time to repay him." The first year he gave away $400—even with only $600 in the bank.

Perhaps the best part of the story is that this generous giver went back to Mississippi to pay a surprise visit to the man who had given him a second chance. The diner owner was retired, and his wife wasn't well. The businessman said the $20 this man had given him when he was down seemed like $10,000 at the time—"so that's exactly how much I paid him back."

I'm confident that if you were to ask the Kansas City "secret Santa," he would tell you that he lives for those moments during Christmas when he can make people's holidays brighter and give the needy some new hope through his gifts. It's a terrific example of what living to give is all about.

This is the lifestyle that we as Christians are called to live out every day of the year. The reason we can live to give is that God has given to us so generously first. So Paul wrote this word of instruction to us:

As for the rich in this present age, charge them not to be haughty, nor to set their hopes on the uncertainty of riches, but on God, who richly provides us with everything to enjoy. They are to do good, to be rich in good works, to be generous and ready to share. (1 Timothy 6:17–18)

Now before anyone objects, "I'm not rich, so I guess I'm off the hook," let me remind all of us that we are rich compared to the rest of the world. And besides, the New Testament's teaching on generous giving is for all believers, regardless of financial status. We serve a God "who richly provides us with everything to enjoy." And one of His most amazing promises is found in Philippians 4:19, which is where we are ending our study of how to be fit for life: "And my God will supply every need of yours according to his riches in glory in Christ Jesus."

This promise is so incredible, we could stop on almost every word. The giver is our God, and the extent of the supply is without limit. Our first thought usually goes to material and financial needs, but I believe this promise extends to any need we could possibly have—physical, spiritual, material, emotional, psychological, marital, family, etc. God is interested in every part of your life.

And because God loves you, His supply is not a trickle of blessing here and there but is "according to his riches in glory in Jesus Christ." That is, God's giving is in keeping with His wealth that is stored up for those who know Christ. The man in our opening story is a good example of "according to" giving. Having $600 in the bank is hardly anybody's idea of financial security, but he gave away two-thirds of it and was obviously blessed in return.

Some people will read a verse like Philippians 4:19 and get out their calculators, so to speak, to figure up how much they can expect from God. Every time I teach on a subject like this, I have to add the caution that this is not prosperity, "name it, claim it" theology. God does not hand us a blank check and invite us to fill in the amount so all of our selfish wishes and dreams will be fulfilled.

We need to understand that behind every *promise* of God is a *premise*. The premise is the biblical context in which that promise occurs and the conditions that may surround it. This is true for Philippians 4:19. It is an astounding promise from God that is as true as His character. But this verse does not float out in space on its own. Verse 19 is embedded in the context of chapter 4, which will help us understand what it means. And more importantly, understanding the context helps us line up our lives with the conditions so that we can experience the overflowing provision of God.

LIVING TO GIVE MEANS THAT WE WILL LIVE EXPECTANTLY

I want to emphasize again that God is not our "secret Santa" who stands ready to meet all of our wants and wishes. But having said that, the fact remains that many times we expect too little of God. Part of the context for the promise of Philippians 4:19 is verse 6, which tells us not to worry about anything but to pray about everything, and then to rest in God's peace knowing that He will answer.

We Need to Make Sure We Don't Short-circuit the Process

That sounds great, but many of us struggle with the process because deep down we don't really expect God to do much of anything. We pray like believers, but then we worry like unbelievers when the answer doesn't come on our timetable.

Let me give an example. Rather than asking God in faith and waiting on Him to provide, many times we just pick up our credit cards and go out and get what we want when we want it. I'm convinced that many believers can't live to give because they are in such debt. And as we are going to see below, when giving takes a backseat to other things in our lives, we short-circuit God's promise by violating the premise. We need to reverse this cycle. I like what one person said: "I will pray for it before I pay for it."

The problem of running ahead of God in this matter of trust is really a problem of too-low expectations. But it's a tragedy to lower our expectations when Jesus gave us this incredible assurance: "Ask, and it will be given to you; seek, and you will find; knock, and it will be opened to you" (Matthew 7:7). The force of the verbs here is tremendous: "Ask, and keep on asking; seek, and keep on seeking; knock, and keep on knocking."

With this kind of offer on the table, it would be a shame to settle for the little bit that we can do in our strength. Someone may say, "Jack, I'd really love to trust God and take Him at His Word. But it's so hard to wait on Him when the bills are coming in every day." I hear you, and so did Paul. That's why another piece of the context in Philippians 4 is verse 13: "I can do all things through him who strengthens me."

God's strength and grace and power are available to help us do anything, but the opposite is also true. That is, I can't do anything apart from Him who strengthens me. Jesus said that Himself in John 15:5: "Apart from me you can do nothing." Some people are not experiencing God's best because they're too busy trying to scratch out a living, just doing the best they can under the circumstances and trying hard to grin and bear it. But Jesus said we can't do anything apart from Him. And the corollary of that is that we won't receive much apart from Him either.

Our Challenge Is to Elevate Our Expectations

Jesus told us to ask Him for our needs. But people often wonder why we have to ask since God knows our needs ahead of time. I don't know all the reasons for that. I just know that the Bible urges us again and again to bring our requests to God. I think a lot of it has to do with the fact that when we ask expectantly and truly trust God for the answer, we put ourselves in a position of faith that pleases Him. I can say on the authority of God's Word that when we pray expectantly, we can be confident that God will hear and answer in His time and wisdom.

What I'm saying is to elevate your expectations! Believe God for great things in your life. And if you need to start small, start by praying what Jesus taught us to pray in His model prayer: "Give us this day our daily bread" (Matthew 6:11).

Life doesn't get much more basic than our daily food. This prayer had an entirely different meaning for Jesus' hearers because in those days workers were paid by the day and had to have the money to buy food for their families each night.

It may seem like a small thing today to ask God for our daily food when our refrigerators and pantries are full. But prayer is an admission of our dependence on God and our recognition that without Him we can't even put food on the table. Prayer also helps us keep our eyes on Jesus, the Supplier of our needs, instead of on the problems and pressures around us. God's provision is available when you ask, so don't limit what Jesus wants to do in your life.

LIVING TO GIVE MEANS THAT WE WILL LIVE CONTENTEDLY

A second premise to the promise of God's supply in Philippians 4:19 is that we must learn to live contentedly. Since the previous chapter was devoted to the issue of contentment, let me just add a few thoughts here.

We Can Be Content and Also Live with Purpose

First, contentment is not laziness. It's not as though we're to live without purpose. Paul himself had holy ambitions; he had a driving compulsion to tell the good news of Christ. The word he used for contentment (v. 11) was used in the secular world to speak of a self-sufficiency that did not need outside assistance. Of course, Paul's sufficiency was not in himself but in Christ. That's why he could say he was content.

We also saw earlier that Paul had to *learn* contentment (v. 11), just as we must. He says in Philippians 4:12 that he had experienced just about every condition known to man. He knew how to be up and how to be down, how to live with and how to live without. The secret is that he was not dependent on his circumstances for his contentment.

He didn't need outside help to be happy because he had the infinite resources of Jesus Christ living within him.

We are naturally malcontented and discontented people. That's why a baby will keep you up all night if he doesn't get what he wants. When our grandson Ian was about six months old, his parents were keeping him and other kids in the nursery at church when Ian saw another child with a toy he wanted. So he crawled over, reached up, grabbed that other baby's cheek, and squeezed it as hard as he could.

Ian's parents didn't teach him to do that, and I can assure you his grandfather didn't either. He did that totally on his own. You don't have to teach a child to be selfish because we are naturally selfish and inclined to want more and more. Some Christians are still childish in this area, always wanting what the other person has. No matter what you have, if you compare yourself to others it will never be enough.

It doesn't matter whether the neighbors refinance or upgrade to a wall-sized, flat-screen television or whatever. The secret to contentment has never changed, and it is this: you don't own anything, and neither do I. Everything we have is a gift from God, from the air we breathe to the food we eat. Even our children are on loan to us from God. We are simply the managers, or stewards, of the good things God has given us temporarily. It all belongs to God, and He gives it to us according to His will and His timetable. And let me remind you and myself that God is not going to subsidize our addiction to money or to anything else.

God doesn't give us everything we want, and for that we can be grateful. Thank God for unanswered prayer at times, when God did not choose to give what we wanted but something far better. But the premise to the promise of God's abundant supply is that if you're going to live contentedly, you're going to trust God to give you what He desires and will be content with His supply.

LIVING TO GIVE MEANS THAT WE WILL LIVE GENEROUSLY

I want to spend the rest of the chapter on this issue because it occupied a good part of Philippians 4 and thus makes a fitting conclusion to this book. I want you to see that the promise of God's abundant supply in Philippians 4:19 is rooted solidly within the context of generous giving. Thus the premise is that living to give means being generous in our giving.

Paul had a special word of commendation for his generous-hearted friends in Philippi who invested in the advancement of the kingdom through his ministry and gave eagerly out of their poverty (2 Corinthians 8:1–4) so that Paul's needs would be met. He said to these believers, "I rejoiced in the Lord greatly that now at length you have revived your concern for me. You were indeed concerned for me, but you had no opportunity" (Philippians 4:10).

The word "revived" means to flourish or flower like a tree bearing fruit. Far from being tight-fisted or reluctant givers, the Philippians were storing up their generous gifts, just waiting for the opportunity to send them to Paul.

Then after speaking of his contentment in Christ, Paul commented further on this matter of giving: "You Philippians yourselves know that in the beginning of the gospel, when I left Macedonia, no church entered into partnership with me in giving and receiving, except you only. Even in Thessalonica you sent me help for my needs once and again. Not that I seek the gift, but I seek the fruit that increases to your credit" (4:15–17). The Philippians were exemplary in their giving, and in the process of thanking them Paul enumerated several principles that are key to understanding the ministry of giving.

Our Gifts Are a Fragrant and Pleasing Offering to God

Paul used several terms to describe the ministry of giving. One is "fruit," as we read above. I want to come back to this one later because it teaches us an important truth about both giving and receiving.

Paul also described the Philippians' gifts as "a fragrant offering, a sacrifice acceptable and pleasing to God" (v. 18). This is a reference to the sacrifices that the Old Testament Israelites brought to God to be offered on His altar. As the aroma of the sacrifice lifted into the air, God said that He smelled it and was pleased. Our tithes and offerings are like a sacrifice to God that He is pleased with because it represents our commitment to Him.

I appreciate the imagery Paul used of "fruit" to describe our giving.

This speaks of the process of sowing and reaping and the law of the harvest. Basically he is saying, if you have a need, plant a seed.

I received a good education in what this means when Deb and I went to pastor a church in southwest Oklahoma early in our ministry. Nearly everybody there was a wheat farmer, and we learned how important it was to reap a crop because every summer, the tithes and the offerings of the church were dependent upon that wheat harvest. I watched as those farmers planted seeds, cultivated the crops, waited for the rain, prayed for the harvest, and then reaped the results.

Just as physical laws go into effect when you plant a seed and produce a crop, spiritual laws of sowing and reaping apply as well. This law says that we reap *what* we sow, we reap *more* than we sow, and we reap *later* than we sow. When you sow apples you reap apples—but it wouldn't be profitable if you didn't reap more than you sow. An apple seed doesn't yield one apple but an entire tree. And the more seeds you plant, the more trees you will get.

That's why Paul uses this idea of planting a seed when we have a need to demonstrate that we reap according to the way we sow, whether "sparingly" or "bountifully" (2 Corinthians 9:6). It is a very simple principle in the Word of God. The law of the harvest says that if we live to give, God will provide not only what is sufficient to meet our needs, but our resources will be multiplied in Christ. Generous giving is the premise behind the promise of Philippians 4:19; so now let's apply it.

God Designed Us to Be Givers and Not Just Takers

God made us to be givers. We live to give, not like a stagnant swamp just taking in and never giving out, but rather like a flowing river as God pours His goodness into our lives. As He floods our lives with blessing, we keep flowing and giving so that others may experience that blessing as well.

I hope you know you don't have to be financially well off to be a generous, gracious giver. If God gives you time, then plant your seed of time, investing in the lives of others and in service to Christ. If God gives you love, then invest that love in the lives of others. If God gives you compassion, then use that gift to touch as many other people as you can.

If you do this, you won't have to worry about running out of time, love, compassion, or anything else because God's supply is endless.

But when the focus of my life becomes me and what I want, life gets very, very small. Some Christians think that because they don't have much, they don't have much to give. But the testimony of the Philippian believers disproves that idea. According to 2 Corinthians 8:1–3, these people were in deep poverty, and yet it was out of their poverty that they gave so cheerfully and generously.

Those early Christians were impoverished, but they were rich toward God, and so they sowed their seed into the life and ministry of Paul. And as a result God said He would supply all of their needs in keeping with the riches of Christ. When I hoard up for myself the blessings of God, I end up either using them on myself or losing them, and I have nothing left to show for it. But when I give of myself and my goods, when I reach out to others and touch them in the love of Jesus Christ, that is an investment that lasts forever.

Learn to Be Others-Focused Even When You Have a Need

If you have a need in your life, the best thing you can do is to turn it over to the Lord and turn your attention to others who have needs so you can minister to them. If you want love, give love and it will come back to you. If you want joy, give joy and joy will come back to you. That's the way it works in God's family because of the law of sowing and reaping.

Many Christians will say, "When God starts blessing me, then I will give and be a blessing to others." But that kind of thinking is completely backwards. You need to give as God has prospered you now, even if it's just a little bit, and as you give and demonstrate your trust in God, He will bless you so that you can give more.

The Bible talks about this principle in many places. God spoke to Israel about their need to fast, but not merely by denying themselves food. It was a different kind of fast that God wanted to see:

Is not this the fast that I choose: to loose the bonds of wickedness, to undo the straps of the yoke, to let the oppressed go free, and to break every yoke? Is it not to share your bread with the hungry and bring

the homeless poor into your house; when you see the naked, to cover
him, and not to hide yourself from your own flesh? (Isaiah 58:6–7)

God is saying that if we want to be spiritual and please Him, the
fast we need to choose is to meet people at the point of their need. This
is what God has called us to do, and notice the promise that follows:
"Then shall your light break forth like the dawn, and your healing shall
spring up speedily; your righteousness shall go before you; the glory of
the LORD shall be your rear guard. Then you shall call, and the LORD
will answer; you shall cry, and he will say, 'Here I am'" (vv. 8–9).

When we choose to minister God's love and grace into the lives of
hurting people, God says, "I'm going to heal your body, strengthen your
soul, and brighten your life; and when you call upon Me in the time
when you need Me the most, I will be there with all of My presence and
all of My provision to supply your every need."

We Will Never Be Able to Outgive Our Great God

We can't outgive God! That's much more than a cliché because His law
of the harvest is in operation. Ecclesiastes 11:1–2 advises us to give generously and spread out our gifts because "you know not what disaster
may happen on earth" (v. 2). In other words, there will be a time in your
own life when you're going to face risks and problems, when you're
going to need somebody to lift you and encourage you and bless you. If
you have been lifting and encouraging others and investing in the work
and the things of God, He will see that you are supplied with what is
necessary in your time of need.

Some people may think this doesn't apply to them because they
have everything going for them and they don't seem to have any needs.
But God has a way of turning things around for the self-sufficient to
teach them how poverty-stricken they really are without Him. This
even applies to believers who are hoarding their blessings and taking in
without ever giving out. We are made to give, not to get.

The Giver Is Also Blessed by His Giving

There's another important principle of giving in Philippians 4:17. We
read it earlier: "I seek the fruit that increases to your credit."

Did you know that the giver is the biggest beneficiary of his own giving? Not only does your giving bless others on earth and bring glory to God, but He stores it up in heaven as your eternal reward! Everything we give to God, even the smallest widow's mite or a cup of water, is headline news in heaven. Everything you do in terms of blessing others and giving your life away will grow your account in heaven.

God is keeping a record; He knows what we give. You may say, "Well, I've been giving and giving, and I haven't been receiving much." Just wait! Just keep on giving and trusting God. Keep sharing your time and talents and treasure in His service, for the Bible says, "Let us not grow weary of doing good, for in due season we will reap, if we do not give up" (Galatians 6:9).

Don't Let the Enemy Rob You of the Joy of Giving

Why do you think there is so much resentment and resistance to the idea of giving among God's people? Pastors just mention money and some people get all bent out of shape. You've heard folks complain, "All they ever talk about at that church is money." But if the promises and the provision of God are so incredible, why is there so much negativity about giving?

Well, think about this. The devil knows that if he can steal the joy of giving out of our hearts, he can defeat us. But don't allow Satan's lies to keep you from experiencing the freshness and fullness and fruitfulness of a life that is given out freely to Christ and others.

Some people have said to me, "I can't afford to tithe." My answer is, you can't afford not to tithe if you want to be blessed. Paul said he was writing these things to the Philippians not because he needed their gifts, but to give them the opportunity to lay up blessing in their heavenly accounts.

What I'm talking about is the principle of first things first. Jesus said, "Seek first the kingdom of God and his righteousness, and all these things will be added to you" (Matthew 6:33).

God has promised to meet every need in your life as you put Him first. But if you're a greedy getter rather than a grateful giver, if you're constantly taking in and never giving out, if you don't give your tithes and offerings to Christ and to His church, if you don't give your time and your talents to serve God, then Jesus is not first in your life.

If you want to be blessed in your family, your career, your finances, your health, and in every other way, put Jesus Christ first in your life. Trust in Him. Give of yourself, and watch God work.

One of my heroes in the ministry was the late Dr. Stephen Olford. I want to close with a quote from Dr. Olford that is appropriate and eloquent:

> It has become apparent that the true measure of yieldedness to the Lordship of Christ is the measure of our discipline and devotion in Christian stewardship. We can talk until doomsday about being surrendered Christians, but we virtually lie until we give evidence of our surrender through stewardship. And make no mistake about it, when we stand before the judgment seat of Christ to render an account of our stewardship we will wish that we had given more since it is inescapably true that what we spend we lose and what we keep will be left to others and what we give away will remain forever ours.

How true. What you spend you lose, and what you selfishly save somebody else will get in the future. But what you give to the work of Christ and the proclamation of the gospel will last forever. There's no better way to be fit for life!